This is Why We Can't Have Nice Things

(PARENTING. MARRIAGE. MADNESS)

CLINT EDWARDS

ISBN: 978-1-4834-3333-2 (sc)
ISBN: 978-1-4834-3334-9 (e)

Lulu Publishing Services rev. date: 09/25/2015

For Mel:

When I said that I loved you more than the kids, you said, "I know."
When I asked if you felt the same about me, you said, "No."
Thank you for your honesty, for reading my drafts, for
insisting that I can, and for Tristan, Norah, and Aspen.

"I remember when my brother and I were playin' in the livin' room and knocked over the table and broke daddy's Jack Daniels Elvis decanter. Shoulda seen Mama. 'We just can't have nice thangs!'"

- Jeff Foxworthy

CONTENTS

Babies

Marriage

NOTE TO READER

While writing this book of essays, I bought a house, had a baby, and lost my mind.

Buckle up.

Thank you to all who helped support this book through my Kickstarter campaign. Your contributions made this possible.

I love you.

No, really. I love you.

Some of these essays/lists appeared in *The Washington Post, The Huffington Post, ScaryMommy,* and *Thought Catalog.*

INTRODUCTION

I was at the doctor when a nurse with five children and a dozen or so grandchildren told me that it goes by too fast. "I'm sure you hear that all the time, but it's true," she said.

I do hear that all the time. And it's true. It seems like yesterday I was standing over the crib as a new father. I was 22, and it was Tristan's first night home with us. He looked so small, swaddled and sleeping, and all I could think about was how my life was going to change in ways I couldn't define. I felt nervous about being a father, and I didn't know just what to do about it. But I knew it was too late to turn back.

My life changed.

It is still changing.

In the moment, parenting is stressful and chaotic, and then, once it's calm, you feel like you lost something. You miss how snuggly your baby was or how hilarious your toddler could be. With each stage in parenting, I've longed to be in another because I couldn't function during the day with my baby waking me in night. Or I was frustrated with fits or tired of fighting during bedtime. And in those moments, I should've slowed down and let it sink in, enjoyed the moment rather than longing for the next stage because I assumed it would be easier.

That's what I was trying to do by writing this book. I was trying to slow down these moments in my life, live them again, get frustrated, and fall in love with my family once more. And maybe, just maybe, by reliving my time as a father and husband, I can now slow down and enjoy what's happening right now. And maybe after reading this book, you will, too.

TODDLER AND GRADE SCHOOL YEARS

CONFESSIONS OF A STAY-AT-HOME DAD

It was a Friday and my feet hurt when I got home, so I kicked off my shoes. The sink was full, the laundry wasn't folded, and the floor was filthy. While passing the kitchen table, I stepped on Lucky Charms and goldfish crackers.

I put my shoes back on.

Most evenings the house was a mess. But this would change in a few days when I took over at home. I was confident. Cocky, even. We lived in a small, stuffy, air-condition-less third floor apartment with three bedrooms and a shady four-foot wide deck that overlooked the Corner Mart in Small Town, Oregon. Sometimes on really hot nights we opened all the windows and fired up the box fans to circulate the stale air, but that mostly wafted in the smell of the first floor family's charcoal grill, so we only did it sparingly. We shared a wall with a pot smoking, 40-something man that regularly participated in loud sex with a leathery woman who cried out in Italian.

We'd just downsized.

We'd lived in the apartment for about six months, and the plan was to live there for a year and save up for a house. The tight space made even little messes eyesores. Cereal bowls sat on the table while toys, random clothing, Spiderman underwear, and more toys covered the living room floor. It wasn't dirt as much

1

as it was kid clutter. Mel had been a stay-at-home mom for about three years, and in our old, larger townhome, it didn't seem as bad. But with the heat and the smaller apartment, the messes seemed worse than ever.

I picked up Norah, my four-year-old, and she smelled like piss. It was all down her legs and along the back of her dress.

"Babe. Norah had an accident." That was what we said in our house. Accident. We didn't say piss. Or poop. Or shit.

We called shit a "code brown."

"Ugh, Norah," Mel said. "That's the second time today." She looked at me. "Can you please just take care of it? I'm trying to make dinner and the kids are driving me nuts. I'm about to kill them." She paused for a moment, looked me in the eyes, and said it again, slowly. "KILL THEM."

Most evenings she talked about murder. Each time it was to emphasize how horrible the kids had acted, and I'd always assumed that it was more of a reflection of her than the kids. I couldn't understand what happened during the day that made her want to murder her own children.

Mel was short and slender with brown hair and thick, brown glasses. We both had thick-framed glasses, and I suppose this was an example of us growing together. We didn't wear glasses before marriage, but now we both did. After nearly ten years, our humor was similar. Our diets were similar. Our taste in TV, books, and movies were similar. After turning 30, my metabolism had really slowed, so I'd started developing an A-cup. With Mel hauling around the kids all day, she'd developed really solid, almost masculine, biceps. Sometimes I wondered if we were slowly becoming the same person.

I wanted to say something about the messy house. I wanted to release the Republican. The *Fox News*-watching asshole that seems to be my default state. The grumpy man of the 1950s that I've tried so hard to put behind me. The man my father was. I was always surprised by how quickly I forgot that Mel worked full-time while I finished school. That she managed the money because of my incompetence with numbers. That she put together all the cheap particleboard furniture I could hardly afford because I was a moron when it came to tools. Instead of saying something poignant and rude, putting her in her place, voting on laws to control her ovaries, giving her the back of my hand, I grumbled a few F-bombs and in a few hours we all had dinner.

Tristan was six, short for his age with a barrel chest and buzzed hair. We had the same slender hands and flat feet. For Halloween he wanted to be a "karate chopper." He liked to use me for practice, turning my shins black and blue. He preferred to be called Tristan Gooey Mac-Flip Edwards, a name he received off a package of mac and cheese. He played Pokémon, watched Pokémon, talked about Pokémon, and dreamed about Pokémon. The more I watched the show with him, the more I wondered if it was teaching him how to train animals to fight for sport. I dreaded getting a call from his future self, informing me that he'd moved to Mexico and started a cock-fighting venue.

At dinner he asked me a bullshit question about Pokémon. "What is Pikachu plus Bulbasaur?"

"I have no idea," I said. "Two?"

"Charmeleon," he said. Then he rolled his eyes like I was a moron.

"What did you learn in school today?" I asked. He said he didn't remember.

Tristan could tell me the damage on nearly any Pokémon. He knew the water types, air types, and electric types. He knew their backstories and their homelands. And yet, if I asked him about school, his day, anything other than Pokémon, he said he couldn't remember. This frustrated the hell out of me. It made me want to build a time machine, go back a few decades, and kill the inventor of Pokémon. But what I think angered me the most was that I

3

didn't feel I could connect with him in any other way than to talk about Pokémon. I thought about how wonderful it would be if the two of us could talk about the news or politics or literature. But he was six. So he told me about Pokémon while I rolled my eyes, nodded, and thought about time travel.

Norah was short and slender with blue green eyes and wavy brown hair, traits she received from her mother. If I called her cranky, Norah stomped her foot and said, "No! I just Norah." She answered to "Goober Baby" and "The Little." She had a fat, round tummy that I loved to tickle. At the time, she was obsessed with puppies, kitties, and babies. And, most importantly, not Pokémon.

I asked about her day, and she barked like a dog.

"I don't speak puppy," I said.

She barked a few more times. Then, in gruff dog-speak, she told me her name was Ringo and began to talk about Ringo in the third person.

"Ringo wants a hug."

"Ringo loves Daddy."

"Ringo wants to play fetch."

"Ruff! Ruff!"

She climbed down from her chair, walked on all fours, and licked my leg. I patted her head, called her a good dog, and told her to get back in her seat.

One of the things I hated most about being a traditional nuclear family was that I didn't really know my kids. At least not like Mel did. I didn't know the names of Tristan's and Norah's friends, which stuffed animals they preferred, or if they liked their toast cut in squares or triangles. Worse yet, I didn't know if they really liked *me*. I looked at Tristan and Norah at the dinner table, and I wondered if we would grow stronger over the summer.

That night, Mel and I discussed the big change that was about to happen in a few days. This was my first summer after graduating with an MFA. I was lucky enough to land a job at a university.

This, in turn, meant that I got the summer off. Mel would be going to school full-time and working an internship over the summer. We were switching roles. I was to be a stay-at-home dad.

In bed we discussed the logistics one more time—when she would leave, when she would be home, and when she would do homework. She reminded me about library day, Norah's dance class, swimming lessons, and our grocery budget.

As she spoke, I thought about sex and how we could be having it. Then I looked at the clock, realized that it was after 10:30, and knew that it wasn't going to happen. Sex never happened after 10:30 anymore. So I drifted back to the Republican. All I could think about was how clean the house would be. How I would not put up with the kids' shit. How I, with a strong hand, would teach those kids how to clean and study and respect me. I honestly felt confident that I could do a better job.

"Are you even listening to me?" she asked.

"Yeah," I said. "Don't worry. I'm confident that the kids will be better fed, smarter, and the house will be cleaner by the end of the summer." I said it sarcastically, like I was joking. But there was just enough honesty in my voice that she felt the bite.

Mel looked at me. "Really? Really? I just hope they don't die."

We turned our backs to each other and turned out the lights.

During the first few days, I demon-cleaned. I vacuumed, scrubbed toilets, washed dishes. I showed Tristan and Norah how to make their beds, clean the living room, and clean the playroom. I expected it of them. I only let them eat healthy things for lunch— peanut butter sandwiches, mandarin oranges, oatmeal, and baked chicken. My life was a checklist. I was going to clean the tub, and once the tub was clean, I wouldn't have to worry about it for some time. I mean, really, how dirty could a tub get? It was soaking in soap most of the time. I felt this way about most of what I was working on. I vacuumed under the kitchen table and assumed that I would only have to do that once every two or three days. Same with the dishes, the laundry, and the playroom. And for the first few days it worked. The kids listened to me.

Mel came home to a tightly run ship, and I looked at her smugly, lip curled. I wanted her to see how wonderfully I was doing. I wanted her to know that I was the master of this house. The best stay-at-home dad ever!

And she admitted it, too.

"Wow!" she said. "The apartment looks great. Good luck keeping it up."

She gave me a shit-eating smirk. *Good luck indeed!* I thought. *You just watch, little miss. Good luck. This will be the cleanest summer in history!*

Day four started out just like the previous three, but then shit started to go off the rails. We got up, had breakfast, got dressed, and around 9:30 a.m., we started picking up the living room. Tristan put his Pokémon cards away, and I asked Norah to pick up her shoes.

"Ruff. Ruff," she said. She was on all fours, panting, her little butt waving like a tail.

"Norah. We don't have time to be a dog. We need to get things cleaned up so we can go to swimming lessons."

"Ruff. Ruff."

"Listen to me," I said. "We don't have time for this. We only have forty-five minutes to do our chores before swimming lessons. Just pick up your shoes."

She barked at me again, and suddenly I got really irritated. More irritated than ever before with one of my kids. Didn't she understand that we had a limited amount of time? Didn't she know that after swimming lessons was dance class? This was the only time we had to clean. So much rode on this. One messy day and Mel would assume she'd won. She'd come home, see the toys in the living room, the food on the floor, and the dirty dishes and conclude that I had fallen short.

Unacceptable.

I asked her again—only this time, with more force.

"Norah. Pick up your shoes. It is not that hard. You're not a dog. You are a little girl with hands. Pick up your shoes, walk on your hind legs, and put them away." I cannot believe I said hind legs, but it made sense at the time.

"Ringo wants to play fetch."

"Ugh…" I yelled. I clinched my fists at my sides.

"She's just being a dog," Tristan said. "You don't have to get so angry."

Now Tristan was back in the room, sitting on the sofa, watching, and not cleaning.

"This doesn't concern you," I said.

Tristan looked me up and down and laughed long and hard, his small hands over his stomach. I looked down and Norah had her shoe in her mouth.

"Oh…kid!" I said. "Don't put it in your mouth. That's disgusting."

I tugged at the shoe, and she clenched down with her jaw, holding it and growling. I have no idea where she learned how to do this. We don't even have a dog.

Norah and I fought over the shoe for some time. I grew more frustrated with the wasted time, yet she enjoyed her time as a dog.

A mix of anger, frustration, and irritation came over me. I picked her up, jerked the shoe from her mouth, carried her down the hall, and tossed her on her bed. My tense body, the anger in my face, the way I threw her onto the bed, everything about that moment showed that I was angry. Norah had to have known that I meant business. But instead of saying she was sorry, instead of falling in line, she laughed. High, happy, child-like laughter that showed she was having a great time. Then she asked if I would throw her on the bed again.

I slammed her bedroom door and walked away. She screamed in her room for nearly 10 minutes. I tried to get things cleaned up, but it was hard to focus with her tormented cries echoing across the apartment.

"She just wants to come out," Tristan said. "You're kind of being a butt." He had his hands on his hips, face soft and stern. He looked a lot like his mother does when questioning my parenting.

That evening Mel came home to a messy house, an irritated husband, and whiny children. She walked through the kitchen, into the living room, her eyebrows raised. "Rough day?" she asked.

"We had a little setback because of Ringo the dog," I said. "But I will get things back in order by tomorrow."

Mel made a clicking sound. "That Ringo has ruined several of my days. Did you put Norah in her room?"

"Yes," I said.

"Did she never stop screaming?"

"Yes."

"I find things go a lot smoother if you just spend a little time listening to her."

"I didn't have time to listen to her. We needed to get going."

"Hmmm," she said. "Let me know how that works out for you."

I scowled.

The next day I decided to one-up Mel. I cleaned the apartment and took the kids hiking.

Our first hiking adventure went great. The kids were excited to do something new. We saw a bald eagle, some ants eating a dead mouse, unidentified animal poop, and a waterfall. The kids loved it!

Mel was impressed by the clean apartment and how I'd managed to get the kids to exercise.

I started taking the kids on a couple hikes a week. Eventually they became more like death marches. Tristan and Norah constantly asked when it would be over and if I could carry them. They dragged their little feet and sagged their shoulders. One of them was always hungry, tired, or thirsty. Norah constantly needed to pee while Tristan always needed to poop. Once Norah wet her pants and sat down in the dusty trail, covering her pants with piss-soaked mud. Then she insisted that I put her on my shoulders.

Tristan called me mean and told me how he'd be happier at home playing the iPad, the Wii, or Pokémon. Watching Netflix would be better.

"Ugh...Dad!" Tristan said. "Let's just go home. This place is stupid."

I told him that those brain-sucking, ridiculously crappy video games had nothing on God's great outdoors.

He called me a butt.

Once we made it to our destination, whether it be a view of the city or a staircase waterfall, Tristan whined until we turned around, while Norah tugged at my pants to proudly show me her wet crotch.

I needed some peace and quiet and thought just maybe I could get that in the bathroom. *Nope.* Even the restroom wasn't private. Every time I went, Tristan and Norah came storming in demanding a popsicle or an argument be settled or to simply stare at what I was doing, confused and amused, as if my business was obviously their business. They pointed, asked questions, made assumptions, but mostly they just laughed. I started locking the door, and that worked for a few days. But then I looked below the door and saw little fingers sticking out beneath it.

"Dad! Can you see my fingers?" my son said, followed by both of them giggling.

Eventually the kids got wise and started anticipating my restroom visits. I'd go to shut the bathroom door and suddenly a small hand or foot would block it. I'd yell at them to leave. I'd threaten to ground them. But it didn't matter. I had to go and they wanted in. It was no use to fight. They forced themselves in for the show.

One night after a hike to the waterfall, Tristan was crying because I'd taken the iPad away, and Norah had pee in her pants. The floor was coated in Cheerios, crackers, clothing, shoes, board games, and DVDs. The tub had a ring. The apartment smelled of rotten milk. I was at the table, head down, massaging my temples.

"I am going to kill them," I said. I looked up at Mel and said it again, slowly. "KILL THEM."

Mel didn't grumble like I used to. She didn't roll her eyes. She didn't swear under her breath. Instead, she looked at me with compassion. Her eyes seemed to say *you've hit bottom. You have given up all hope. And with that change, we will rebuild you and make you stronger.*

She rubbed my back and said, "You're cracking. I get it. I understand."

One month into being a stay-at-home dad, all I did was drink Diet Coke and bitch. My lust for cleaning had dwindled. I started to accept my failure. I ate an alarming amount of ice cream. I allowed the kids to watch movies all day so I could sleep warmly in my bed, away from what my children were becoming...lazy slobs like myself.

It was on one of these resting days that Norah came in with her toy doctor kit. She placed her soft hand on my face and said, "You need a checkup."

She gave me Bun-Bun (her stuffed bunny) to hold. Then she checked my eyes, ears, blood pressure, and temperature. She leaned in close, her face to the side, her eyes peaceful and concerned. I thought about what Mel said earlier in the summer: "I find things go a lot smoother when you listen to them." I started to realize that I was trying to control my kids instead of trying to work with them. I wasn't listening.

"You need a shot," she said. "But it's just a little one. It won't hurt."

She gave me a shot in the leg. Then she raised her arms and said, "All better. You can get out of bed now."

Funny thing was, I did feel a little better. There was sweetness in what she was doing that made me feel hopeful.

When Mel came home that night, I put it all on the table.

"I admit it. I am a horrible father. How do I do it? How do you listen to them?"

She wasn't smug about it. She didn't look me in the face, smile, and tell me that I had only one job and I couldn't do it. She didn't tell me that I was pathetic. I suppose she didn't need to. I was telling myself all those things already. Instead, she sat across from me at the table and said, "Kids can suck sometimes. I mean, you love them. But they can really suck."

"Tell me about it," I said. "Really frustrating."

"I find things go a lot smoother when I just don't worry so much about the house. I just focus on listening to them. Ask them what they want and try to use that to get what you want." She gave me a few examples, like how Norah cleans up the living room a lot easier if you whistle at her and pretend it's a game of fetch. And that Tristan cleans up the play room if you bribe him with candy or tell him he will get a few extra minutes of video games for not complaining.

The two of us really connected that day. I'd spent some time in her shoes, and I think it did me some good. And I think Mel understood me better, too. Near the end of the conversation, I thanked her for the advice. She smiled and said, "Thanks for listening."

Each time I came home and she looked like she was about to crack, it was her way of asking for help. Asking me to give her a break before she broke. It was her way of telling me that raising young children is a non-stop day of whining and bitching and wanting and needing and crying and pissing mixed with an occasional tender moment that makes it all worthwhile. Moments like when Norah gave me a checkup. It's not like a job with a lunch break. It's not something that I could set down on my desk for a moment while I took a walk so I could come back with a fresh head. I finally understood, and I think Mel appreciated my new understanding.

That night we had sex after 10:30.

Things went a little smoother after that. I tried the whistle method on Norah, and it worked. So what if she was carrying everything with her mouth? I didn't care anymore. I knew it was the best way to get things done. Once, when she threw a fit and I had to put her in her room, I thought about her love for animals. I went and got a cow puppet. I sat on her bed with the puppet on my right hand and in my best cow voice I said, "Norah, my name is Dr. Cow. I have a Ph.D. in tickles and hugs. Why are you so sad?"

Norah unloaded on Dr. Cow. She told him how Tristan had scared her by making a funny face. Then he didn't apologize. "He just made me really scared," she said. Then she gave Dr. Cow a hug, and together they went and chatted with Tristan to resolve the problem.

Dr. Cow started making regular appearances. He made things go much smoother with Norah.

Tristan was a tougher nut to crack. I didn't know how to get him to want to talk to me. So I asked him about Pokémon. Only this time, I wasn't negative about it. Instead of trying to force him to talk about something I wanted him to talk about, I got excited about Pokémon and used it as a way to get what I wanted...to better understand my son. I started out by telling him that the toys in the living room were Pokémon and he needed to catch them. He was too smart for that.

"Dad, those are toys. Not Pokémon," he said. "I'm not stupid."

So I tried a few other ploys. I told him that Pokémon trainers eat baked chicken. He didn't believe me. "They eat candy," he said. Then he called me Mr. Fart-fart.

I told him finding Pokémon is easier after taking a bath. They can't smell you coming. He rolled his eyes and said, "No way. Trainers never take baths. They live in the woods."

But I kept at it. And as I did, I realized what I really wanted from him. I wanted him to know how to work and clean and all that. But what I really wanted was to connect with him. Tristan is a funny kid. He has a big personality, like me. But I realized he hid behind his personality by telling jokes and laughing. And if that didn't work, he talked about Pokémon. And when that failed, like it often did with me, he just said, "I don't remember." Everything with him was surface level. He'd never told me about his favorite subjects in school, about his best friend, or if he was starting to notice girls. What I really wanted was for Tristan to open up to me.

So I started reading a little about Pokémon online. Nothing too in-depth, just enough to feel like I could engage in the conversation. I tried hard to shove my hatred of Pokémon deep down inside. And I practiced talking about it without using the words stupid, irritating, or ridiculous (this was difficult, I assure you).

One night as we had dinner as a family, Tristan started talking about Pokémon, and I listened. I asked him about different creatures and trainers. I told him about some of the regions I'd read about. He raised his eyebrows and smiled. We went back and forth.

Then I asked him about his friends at school and which one would make the better Pokémon trainer. I asked him what he learned today that might make him a better Pokémon trainer. He opened up. He told me that Samantha would be the best trainer.

"Why do you say that?" I asked.

"I don't know..." He paused and thought for a moment. "I think because she can run really fast. And she isn't very tall, so she could hide behind bushes. And I just think she is smart and has a funny laugh."

The corners of his mouth twisted, and Mel and I looked at each other with raised eyebrows.

I asked if Samantha was his girlfriend.

"No way," he said. "I just think she's funny. And I like when she smiles. And sometimes she pushes me on the swing."

Then he paused for a moment. "It'd be really fun to catch Pokémon with her."

He folded his arms, put his head down, his cheeks a little flushed, and I knew the conversation was over.

"Samantha does sound like she would be a great trainer," I said.

Tristan smiled. Then he walked to his seat at the table, grabbed his plate, and walked back to me. He hopped on my lap, and we ate like that for the first time in months.

Across the table, Norah told Mel about her new friend Dr. Cow and how he gives really great hugs. Mel smiled, looked at me, and whispered, "Doctor Cow?"

"He has a Ph.D. in tickles and hugs," I said. "They've had a few appointments."

Mel shrugged. "OK."

Books, movies, and toys lined the table. We'd shoved them to the side to make room for our plates. The sink was full of dirty dishes, the floor was sprinkled in cereal, and the living room looked like the stuffed animals had a blowout party. I didn't care. I understood what went into keeping a clean house, and I finally understood that connecting with my family was more important.

I didn't think less of Mel. In fact, I had more respect for her. I understood what she was up against. More importantly, though, I felt like I better understood my kids. And I hoped that they better understood me, too.

THE DAY WE CAUGHT OUR KIDS LOOKING AT THEIR BUTTHOLES

Mel walked into our kitchen wearing jeans and a pink shirt. It was a Friday night—and her 32nd birthday. I'd just placed candles in Mel's cake and was washing my hands at the sink when she approached me.

"I just caught the kids looking at their buttholes. We should talk to them about that."

It took me a moment to figure out what the hell she had just said. I played a scene out in my head where a naked Tristan and Norah bent over and giggled. In my mind, it seemed innocent enough. But the more I thought about it, the stranger it became.

One of my duties as a father was to get the kids ready for bed, which really was a collection of other duties, one of them being herding the kids into the bath. Moments earlier, I'd started filling up the tub in the kids' bathroom and started the shower in the parents' bathroom, and then stepped into the kitchen while Tristan and Norah got undressed. Somehow in the few moments it took me to walk down the hall to the kitchen, our children had decided to explore their butts.

Shit like this was the main reason they bathed separately. About six months ago both kids were in the tub. Mel caught Tristan and

16

Norah play fighting. Tristan was wielding his penis like a weapon, while Norah was holding a rubber ducky like a sword. The rest of the details are sketchy, but from what I understand, the weapons collided. They giggled. Then Mel made Tristan move into the other bathroom. When Mel broke up this ducky-penis fight, Tristan and Norah acted like she was the strange one. Like she was the one who needed decency education.

That day we decided they were too old to bathe together.

Childhood curiosity aside, I felt an obligation as a parent to help my kids understand social decency. It was probably nothing to worry about. But then again, it was downright strange, and I wanted it to stop. I didn't want to be the parent of that dude in Central Park showing strangers his penis. Nor did I want to get an email down the road from someone telling me that my daughter appeared on *Girls Gone Wild*, showing strangers (the world) her butthole. Call me old fashioned, but the last thing I was going to do was encourage genital-to-bath toy play fights or the examination of family butts.

Mel and I stood in the kitchen.

"Hold on," I said. "Say that again."

Mel let out a breath, like what she was saying was an everyday thing and easy to understand, and the fact that I asked her to repeat it made me the fool.

"I was in Norah's room when I overheard Norah say, 'What's that hole in your butt?' Then Tristan said, 'It's my butthole. Want to look at it?' I heard laughter. Once I came into the bathroom, things had obviously progressed because Tristan was now looking at Norah's butthole."

She paused for a moment. Then she said, "We should have a talk with them."

Usually when Mel said, "We should talk with them," she meant should talk with them." Normally I fought this assumption, but I did consider the fact that it was Mel's birthday. I thought about how I'd like to spend my birthday, and I knew that it wasn't handling some strange moment like the one being discussed.

"How exactly do you suggest I handle this?" I said.

I honestly didn't know how to approach this subject. What were the ramifications of it all? What were my kids experimenting with? Was this something that needed to be handled? I never examined any of my siblings' butts. I thought about asking Mel if she ever examined any of hers, but, truth be told, I'd rather not know.

If they weren't brother and sister, that would be one thing. But they were, and that was just strange. I assumed that both were too young for this to be a sexual thing, but at the same time, I didn't really know. It felt like we were moving into some strange new territory as parents, a land filled with brothers and sisters looking at each other's butts. A community I'd rather not be a part of.

"Just go tell them that it's not appropriate and that they shouldn't do it anymore."

Her explanation sounded simple enough, but I knew that it wouldn't be that easy. I wondered if I should speak to them together or separately. I knew that I needed to chat with them tonight, or they would forget about the whole thing. I wondered if I should chat with them while they bathed, if I should wait until we all sat at the table eating birthday cake. I imagined it. Mel blowing out her candles after we sang the happy birthday song. Then we'd all sit around the table and, as we munched on cake, I'd bring up an awkward conversation about buttholes.

For the sake of Mel, I decided to talk to them individually as they bathed.

I thought for a moment before I approached Tristan in the shower. I ran a few heart-felt parenting speeches through my head—ones that I thought would be appropriate to handle such a strange subject. All of them seemed to start with "When a young boy becomes a man..." or "When I was a boy...", but nothing I could think of really fit the complicated subject matter that I was dealing with.

Once I got to my son, all of those long-winded, Tim Taylor-style, life-changing dad speeches went out the window.

"Hey," I said. "Don't look at your sister's butthole."

"Why not?" Tristan asked. He was naked, in the shower. Water was running down his chest, his mouth in a half frown, hands clenched in fists at his sides. He looked offended, like he was a teenager and I'd told him not to smoke pot or suggested he wear deodorant.

Then he started laughing.

Tristan is a complex little guy. When faced with a situation he doesn't like or doesn't understand, he will get angry at first and then try to make a joke to lighten the situation. I did the same thing when I was young, so I understand his logic. But what I didn't understand as a boy was how infuriating it is to try to talk to someone about a serious subject and have the person laugh in your face, or make jokes the whole time.

"It's weird," I said. "Do you ever see me or mom looking at our buttholes?"

Tristan thought about this for a moment, and then he laughed. "I don't know, but that would be really funny if you did."

Rather than linger on what was obviously a bad comparison, I kept talking.

"Do you have friends that do that? Please tell me that you don't have friends that look at your butthole."

"No, I don't," he said.

Then he started laughing harder, and I got worried that I'd just given him an idea. I explained to him that what he was doing was inappropriate and strange, and I didn't want him to do it anymore.

"Fine," he said, rolling his eyes. "I won't look at Norah's butthole anymore."

I wasn't sure if I could believe him, so I said, "Do you promise?"

Tristan let out a long breath. "Yes, Dad!"

"Thank you," I said.

I approached Norah on the subject. She was stretched out in the tub, her head half underwater.

I asked her if she'd looked at Tristan's butthole, and she giggled.

In her chipper, four-year-old voice she cried, "Yup!"

I'm not sure if I laughed because of her response or because the conversation was absurd, but what I do know is that I had to step from the room and regain my composure. I stood in the hallway for a while, listening to her giggle. I was a mix of silly laughter and anxiety, trying to understand if I was handling this situation appropriately.

It is in moments like these that I fully realize what people mean whey they say there is no instruction manual on raising children. Would there be a chapter titled, "How to Approach Your Children About Not Looking at Their Sibling's Butt and Turn It into a Rewarding Moment"? No, I don't think so. How on earth could someone come up with a text complex enough to tackle the unexpected situations that can arise when raising a family?

Once I came back, I told Norah in my best serious voice that what she did was inappropriate and strange, and I asked her to never do it again.

"OK," she said. "I won't ever, ever look at Tristan's butthole ever again."

Norah is at that age where she will say "OK" to just about anything she is confronted with and then ignore it when the opportunity to disobey you presents itself. If I tell her not to steal cookies from the pantry, she will say, "OK." Then I know that there is a 75% chance that I will find her 20 minutes later trying to steal cookies from the pantry. But much like when I discussed this situation with Tristan, I just wanted it to be over.

"Thank you," I said.

After both kids got out of the tub, I sat in the living room and thought about what it meant to be a parent. I wondered if I'd handled this situation well or if I'd just made things worse. I hoped that something like this would never happen again, but I knew that it would.

I never had an awkward talk with a parent. I didn't really know my father that well, and my grandmother half-raised me. I was shuffled between homes a lot, and so I missed out on a lot of those clichéd Hallmark moments, like the birds and the bees talk. But I'd heard a lot from friends talk about their parents approaching them about awkward subjects like the one I faced. My friends always said how it felt like the whole situation was so awkward for them, like all they wanted was for the conversation to just end. But what I never realized was that those conversations are just as awkward for the parents.

Maybe even more so. Especially when I consider how I feel that my children are a reflection of myself.

There is no way I'm going to get out of parenthood without having more awkward conversations with my kids. I just hope that, with time, they will focus on things other than butts.

STOP EATING YOUR BOOGERS AND BE A GENTLEMEN

Tristan ate a booger in front of me. Then he smiled and said, "Mmmmm."

We were in the backyard pulling weeds because Mel asked me to and Tristan volunteered. It was unusual for him to get excited about wanting to both pull weeds and spend time with me.

He'd been going through this pre-preteen phase. Most of the time I embarrassed him. He wouldn't let me hug him in front of his friends. A month earlier, I dropped him off at school. He sprinted from the car, darting in front of the school's heavy morning traffic to keep me from giving him a hug. Part of me hoped he'd have a close call with a car. A near miss or something. I didn't want him to get hurt. I just wanted him to be good and scared so I could lean down, look him in the eyes, and say something like, "Not hugging your dad sometimes means getting hit by a car. It's just the way the universe works." He'd have to believe me because he was seven. But none of that happened. Instead, I just stopped hugging him in public.

It's an unwritten agreement of sorts.

He's pulling away from me, which has made me think a lot about him growing up and moving on. I wonder how much more time I have to influence his life before he sees me as this domineering thing in a polo shirt and cargo shorts, whose advice is old-fashioned and worthless.

"You know, Tristan," I said. "Someday you are going to do that in front of someone you're attracted to. That person is going to call you disgusting, while you are going to think they are cute. It will make you feel so crappy that you won't ever eat a booger again."

I assumed he would tell me that I was lying. That he didn't care who liked him or not, or some other clichéd seven-year-old answer. Instead Tristan looked up at me, hands dirty from pulling weeds, the booger still soaking in his mouth, and said, "Did you ever eat a booger in front of mom?"

I laughed. "I ate a booger in front of a girl on the school bus once. It wasn't your mom. Her name was Liz. I thought this girl was really cute at the time, and I thought eating a booger would make her think I was funny like it did with my older brother. I was probably eleven. I put the booger in my mouth, then I stuck out my tongue and showed it to her. She put her head down and puked in her lap."

Tristan put his hand over his little chubby tummy and laughed long and hard. "That is awesome!" he said.

I laughed a little, too. I couldn't help it. His reaction was priceless.

"Listen, someday you are going to want to date. Someday you are going to meet someone, and you are going to want to impress that person. And maybe, you will find someone that is impressed by boogers and farts and all the other crap you always talk about with your buddies but chances are, they won't be. Someday you are going to move out of this house and go out on your own, and you will have to stop all of this gross booger stuff and find something else to talk about. Something of value. And I don't know what that's going to be, but what I do know is that when your mom and I first got married, I still thought farts and boogers were charming. After two weeks of marriage, your mom and I sat in bed, and I thought it would be really funny to fart and then pull the blanket over her head."

"Why did you do that?" Tristan asked.

I smiled, and then I said, "Because I thought it would be funny to trap her and the fart under the blanket."

Thinking back, I didn't really answer his question because I'm not really sure why I did that to my wife. Growing up with other boys had shown me that farts make friends. Perhaps I did it because for so long I'd gotten used to receiving positive attention from my buddies for talking about farts and boogers.

Once again Tristan wrapped his hand over his stomach and started laughing at the thought of his mother trapped under a blanket with a fart, and for a moment, I felt like I was failing at this whole Ward Cleaver parenting talk.

"Listen," I said. "She didn't think it was funny at all. She squirmed and coughed under there, and when I let her out, I was laughing hysterically. But she wasn't. She started hitting me and calling me a jerk. Then she made me sleep in the living room for a few nights. She was really, really mad." I thought about mentioning that she also cut me off from sex for almost a month, but decided I'd better keep that conversation for another time.

Tristan now listened, both hands in his shorts pockets.

"Someday," I said, "you are going to grow up and be on your own. You will probably get married to someone you really love and respect. And I suppose my advice to you is, don't be gross. Be a gentlemen. Treat your partner with respect. Don't eat boogers in front of them. Don't make them smell your farts because stuff like that will probably make your partner feel like THEY are the kind of person who deserves to be farted on. And that's not a way to make a good relationship work."

Neither of us spoke for a moment. I looked at Tristan's face, and it almost felt like I'd gotten through to him, that my advice for adult life had worked. As a father I don't get to feel this sort of satisfaction all that often, so I didn't say anything. I just savored the moment.

Tristan looked up at me. I expected him to say something important. Something that reflected the change I'd obviously made in his perceptions on adult life.

He took a deep breath and said, "I farted. And it smelled really good." Then he placed his hands over his tummy again and started laughing.

WHY MY DAUGHTER'S TEEN YEARS MAKE ME THINK ABOUT MURDER

Mel had her hair pulled back when she told me about Norah's kiss. She was laughing the whole time. Norah was in Sunday school with the perpetrator. After the children sang "I am a Child of God," Mel noticed that Norah was holding Jonathon's hand. Then she leaned over and kissed him on the cheek.

"It was absolutely adorable!" she said, rising to her heels. "They are so cute!"

I am head over heels for Norah. Sometimes I ask her if she will stay cute and little and love me forever. She always says "Yes!" in a sweet, little voice. Then she rolls her eyes. But I know that it isn't true. Someday I will cramp her style. Someday she will dislike me. I will become an embarrassment. I will stand between her and some dreamy jerk with a nice smile. Someday she will fall in love and leave me, probably much sooner than I'd like, and the thought of that breaks my heart.

This is why when Mel told me Norah kissed Jonathon, a little boy at church, I went cold. I felt a white-hot heat in my stomach. I wanted to go to this boy and let him know that he needed to keep his hands off my daughter.

I knew Jonathon. He was confident with a random sense of humor that I found appealing. In fact, I kind of liked the kid, and I suppose I understood Norah's attraction. I knew his parents. They were good people. His father was a Ph.D. candidate. His mother was sweet and soft-spoken. Their kids had cute blond hair—an all-around good family.

Not long before the kiss, we were at their home playing board games. I should have known something was up with Norah and Jonathon that night.

The adults played Monopoly in the kitchen. I went to check on the kids in the living room. Jonathon danced and sang as Norah sat on a small wooden chair and watched. She clapped every so often and swooned a little, her small butt wiggling to the sound of Jonathon's voice. Jonathon was wearing gym shorts with a Mario Brothers pajama top. Not the wardrobe I'd have picked when impressing a girl, but it seemed to be working for him. In his hand was a long yellow dart with a red suction cup on one end. He used it as a microphone, his hips swinging, right heel pounding out a beat. He kept singing, "I choose you. You. You."

With each "you" Norah put her hand over her mouth or her heart, and she giggled or smiled longingly, the same smile she often gave me when I entered the room after a long absence. I laughed for some time. I didn't really think anything was up, and in fact, there wasn't. I don't think they had any idea what they were doing outside of having a good time. But when I reflect back on my life, some of the worst decisions I've ever made revolved around a good time (like when I took my pants off in a hotel elevator while on a fieldtrip with the Future Farmers Association, or the time I was almost arrested for messing around with my girlfriend in a McDonald's parking lot).

A few hours after Mel told me about Norah's kiss, I sat down next to her on our faded gray sofa. Her hands were curled down like paws, and she was sniffing the armrest and wiggling her bottom like a puppy. I wondered if she'd been acting like a puppy around Jonathon. Was impersonating a dog an attractive quality at the age of four?

Kids are strange.

"Tell me about Jonathon," I said.

"Ruff. Ruff," she replied.

I wondered if she would use this same dog impersonation strategy when she's a teenager to get out of difficult conversations.

"Norah," I said. "I want to know what happened."

Norah sat up, crawled into my lap and licked my arm. Then she began speaking in the third person, like she often did when pretending to be a dog.

"Ringo wants to play fetch."

I told her that kisses are very special things and that she needed to save them for very special boys. She got quiet for a moment, just long enough for me to think that I was getting through to her. Then she looked up at me, smiled, and said, "Ringo farted on your leg."

I wasn't getting anywhere. So I tried a different strategy. I told her that there was something in her mouth. She furrowed her brow, her face a mix of fear and confusion. Her paws straightened out, and she looked up at me.

"What is it?" she asked.

"I'm not sure. Open wider."

She opened her mouth and I let out a confused "Hmmmm."

I told her it was a boy monster. She looked scared as I looked closer.

"Yup," I said. "Definitely a boy monster. The crazy thing about boy monsters is that you can't feel them. You don't even know they are there. But they scare boys away."

It's not too often that I feel this clever. I recall thinking that this was probably the best idea I'd ever had. My chest swelled a little as I told her that boy monsters are the most wonderful thing in the world and that she was really lucky to have one.

"Take it out," Norah said.

"Can't," I said. I searched my mind for a responsible age. An age that I felt was old enough. Mature enough. An age that I could say, "Yeah. Norah is ready to date."

"It has to stay in there until you are twenty-eight years old."

This was only three years younger than I was at the time. It was also six years older than I was when I married Mel.

Norah screamed. It was a long and loud in a pitch that I'd never heard before—the kind of scream I assume Rapunzel let out after being locked in a tower. It scared me. It must have scared Mel, too, because she came running into the living room to see if everything was all right.

"We're fine," I said. "Nothing to worry about here. I just told Norah about the boy monster in her mouth. It's nothing."

Norah started crying at my mention of the boy monster. She asked Mel to take it out. By now Tristan, our six-year-old, had entered the room. Even though he had no idea what a boy monster was, he started laughing at the sound of it.

"Boy monster," he said. "Monsters aren't boys."

Mel furrowed her brow at me, her lips slightly twisted. It was a confused and frustrated look that she often gives me when discovering one of my non-conventional parenting strategies, like the time I suggested we use cold showers to help with potty training, or the time I convinced Tristan to try broccoli because it would give him deadly farts.

I came clean and told her about the boy monster and how it can't be removed until Norah is twenty-eight years old.

"Isn't it wonderful?" I said.

Just the thought of it made me smile.

Norah was now sprawled out on the floor, right hand in her mouth, using her thumb and index finger to root around and pluck out the boy monster. Mel gave me a slack-jawed look that said, *You're a child.* Then she reached in Norah's mouth with two fingers, made a plucking motion, and said, "I got it."

Norah let out a sigh of relief. I grunted with frustration.

Later that night as I loaded the dishwasher, Mel brought up the boy monster. She reminded me about how Tristan was kissed by a little girl at the park about two weeks earlier. We were at Silk Falls with some friends. I was getting a few things at the car, when the daughter of one of our friends leaned over and kissed Tristan on the cheek. Then she ran away, squealing. She had red hair and dimples and was about a year younger and three inches taller than Tristan. He is short like me, always the shortest in his class. I imagine she had to lean down to kiss him, and I assume that Tristan wiped the kiss away soon after.

"What did you do when I told you about that?" she said.

I grunted. I didn't want to respond because I knew just where she was going.

"Oh. You don't remember? I will tell you. You gave him a high five and called him a stallion." She stumbled saying stallion, which seemed to give the word emphasis. Which it deserves. "Then you told him that he takes after you."

"Which he does," I said. Mel stretched out her lips into a duck face and tipped her head to the side, something she often does when I try to show false confidence. It seemed to say, *You wish.*

"I don't understand the difference," Mel said. "Tristan gets a kiss and it's no big deal. In fact, you were happy about it. Norah kisses a boy and you freak out."

Mel was lightly jerking her head side to side like she often did when she knows she's right. I thought about it for a moment. I tried to defend myself with a bunch of false starts.

"But Tristan is a boy…"

"Norah is a girl…"

"Boys only want…"

But logically, none of my arguments added up. I could tell before I even finished saying them.

I stood next to the sink for a while, Mel staring at me, her eyes a mix of anger and curiosity. I tried to make sense of it. I searched deep inside to find a justification for my actions, for my anger about Norah kissing a boy and my thrill about Tristan getting a kiss. But I couldn't find any good reason for it. All of my reactions were knee-jerk. I wanted to protect Norah from predators while I was probably turning Tristan into one.

I looked at the ceiling, exhaled, and said, "I don't understand it either. I'm kind of a dick."

Mel smiled. "Yup," she said.

On Labor Day, we went to a park to barbeque with a large group of friends from church. Jonathon, the kissing boy, was there with his parents. He was dressed like Link from the Legend of Zelda—green pants, a green poncho, a long green hat, and a white shield in one hand and a sword in the other. Norah looked at him dreamily, and then the two went to the playground. Together they rode one of those big green plastic seahorses on a large industrial spring.

The girl that kissed Tristan was there, too. Her name was Susan. She sat on the lip of the sidewalk, elbows on her knees, face in her palms, and gazed at Tristan on the swing. He was screaming in his high-pitched little boy scream, legs kicking randomly, face red and distorted, a clear display of attention whoredom.

I didn't get angry with Norah and I was not proud of Tristan. I just stood there, stared, and accepted the fact that this was happening. I looked at Jonathon dressed as Link and wondered what I would think if Norah came home with a teen boy dressed that way. Then I thought to myself, *Norah. You could do better.*

Then I looked at Susan as she gazed at Tristan. I wondered why Tristan was screaming like a high-pitched girl. I wondered what Susan could possibly see in his obviously goofy desire for attention that everyone else probably thought was obnoxious. I thought to myself, *Susan. You could do better.*

And once again, I was thinking in contradictions. I was seeing men (even my own son) as villains. Perhaps this was the way I was raised to think. Perhaps the media had taught me to view men as sex-driven maniacs ready to deflower sweet little girls. Or perhaps, and I think is more likely, this was a reflection of myself. Sure I needed to protect my daughter. And I needed to teach my son to be a gentleman. But I didn't understand any of that as a kid. And I think the reason I didn't was because my father wasn't around. So I had to learn about being a man, and what that meant, on my own.

Maybe, just maybe, being an example of a good respectable man will help Norah to know what one looks like. She will know how to spot one, and hopefully she will fall in love with someone I can feel comfortable with her marrying. And, in turn, my example will teach Tristan how to treat a girl.

What I really needed to be thinking was, *Clint, you can do better.* I needed to stop worrying about Clint as a hormone crazed teen with little paternal direction and focus a little more on the respectable father and husband I'd been trying to become. Then I needed to find ways to lead my kids by example. Suddenly, I had a mix of fear and hope. Fear because I knew, deep in my heart, that I was prone to dumbass decisions, and there was a good possibility that I might inadvertently screw things up. Hope because I had a plan that seemed reasonable.

Later at the park, Norah came and sat next to me on a park bench. She wrapped her soft hands around my forearm and hugged it like she often did.

"Why aren't you hanging out with Jonathon?" I asked.

She sighed and looked up at me. "He's playing swords with his friends. I don't like that game. It's stupid. I'm just going to sit by you."

I wanted to tell her that loser guys do that. I wanted to warn her. But I didn't. I just put my arm around her, and I kissed the top of her head.

A few moments later, Mel sat on my right side. I put my arm around her, too. I kissed her on the cheek. "I love you."

I looked at Norah. She was watching us with a big smile.

IS SPEAKING BURRITO A PUNISHABLE OFFENSE?

Tristan was talking in Burrito again. It's a language he created. He repeats the word "burrito" over and over again but with influxes in volume and tone. He ends the word a little higher when asking a question. Or he says the word down low, his face looking somber, to show disappointment. And he repeats the word quickly, at a high pitch, when trying to show anger. He thinks this is hilarious.

I do not.

In fact, I find it really irritating. It was 8a.m. on a Saturday, and that was part of the problem. I'd just gotten up. I wasn't in the mood to speak to Tristan in Burrito, but that didn't matter. He was in his Skylanders underwear, bright-eyed and bushy-tailed, tugging at my pants, and pointing at something he wanted, probably the candy on the top of the fridge, and saying, "burrito" over and over and over.

"Tristan," I said. "I'm not in the mood for this. I just got up. Tell me what you want. In English please."

"Burrito," he said.

"Then you get nothing."

He didn't give up. He tugged harder on my pants, almost pulling them off, repeating that stupid word, and pointing, as though I would eventually figure it out. But I didn't figure it out, nor did I want to figure it out. It just all seemed so asinine at the time. I had no idea how speaking in Burrito was going to help him think at a higher level.

The strange thing is, outside of him speaking in Burrito, which is strange by itself, is that he thinks the word is f-ing hilarious. He won't eat a burrito, mind you. He won't eat anything other than ramen noodles, dinosaur-shaped meat, and mac-n-cheese. He also enjoys Lucky Charms, but he really only eats the marshmallows, so I don't fully count that as part of his regular diet.

The most he knows about burritos is that they have been offered to him. He always looks at the burrito with terror, as though it is a long, dark cave, then promptly turns it down. So I don't fully understand where he picked up this Burrito language.

I just know that it drives me nuts, and I often wonder how long it will last. How long will he speak in Burrito? How long will he find this nonsensical language to be hilarious? Is he going to be that kid in high school who answers the question: *What is the capital of New Mexico? Burrito.*

Will he think he is being funny, while in fact he is being offensive?

I looked down at him standing on the kitchen floor, still repeating the word and pointing, and all I wanted to do was put my hands over his mouth. Not out of anger, but out of fear because, frankly, he looked a lot like I did at his age—stocky and blue-eyed, with an obnoxious, dimpled grin. But most importantly, he didn't only remind me of the way I looked at six-years-old but also the way I acted and the irritating things I did in the name of humor—making faces, annoying sounds with my nose, asking people to pull my finger, etc.

I crouched down, looked him square in the eyes, and said, "Tristan. I don't want to hear the word "burrito" again for the rest of the day. Just tell me what you want, in English, and I will get it for you. No matter what it is. This is a free pass. Before you say anything, realize what you have here. You could ask for a box of cookies, and I would get it for you. And you could eat all of it. $100? It's yours. All you have to do is ask in a language I can understand. OK? Do you get what I'm saying right now?"

He paused and gave me a long look, considering which of these amazing requests he planned to take me up on. Finally, I'd gotten through to him.

"Burrito."

He followed the word with a sly smile. His face seemed to say, *I don't care what you have to offer. I'm here for my own amusement, and that is priceless!*

I sent him to his room.

And in that moment, I wondered if speaking in Burrito was a punishable offense. Was I overstepping my bounds as a father?

I didn't know what else to do, and part of me hoped it would change his behavior. But deep down, I knew it wouldn't.

I thought about all the times I got mocked, pushed, and slapped around for being a weirdo. I thought about all the girls that had given smiles that seemed to say, *You're cute.* And then I spoiled the deal by making a funny face or a fart sound with my armpit. And I wondered if he was, somehow, following in my footsteps. And I wondered if putting him in his room could possibly change the poor genes I'd obviously given him.

UNWANTED PARENTING ADVICE AND HOW I'D LIKE TO RESPOND

People regularly give me unsolicited advice on parenting, both in person and online. And you know what? I get it. You think you've figured something out, and you want to share your great revelation. Or perhaps you don't have kids, so that makes you an outside observer with a fresh prospective. But really, I'd rather you just shut the hell up. Below are a few examples of unsolicited advice I've been given and how I would like to respond (if I weren't such a nice guy).

1. Shouldn't he be wearing a jacket? Yup, he probably should be wearing a jacket. And you know what, I don't know when he last changed his underwear or socks, either. But here's the deal. I told him to put on a jacket, but he's seven and he listens about as well as a goldfish. Each evening I wrestle him into the bathtub. I don't have energy for much more, so I'm letting him figure out a few things the hard way, through goose bumps and rashes. Can you live with that? Because I can.

2. You know, breastfeeding is better for babies (I heard this *a lot* with our first baby). No shit, doctor. But let me tell you about real life. My wife had every intention of breastfeeding, and she did for the first month, but then she had to go back to work because her shitty employer only gave her a one-month maternity leave and doesn't provide a place to pump outside of the communal break room and the public restroom. Sadly, most people think breastfeeding is about as socially acceptable as public urination. Hooking up to a breast pump while her coworkers enjoy a tuna fish sandwich would definitely be unwelcome. So Mel decided it would be better to use formula. Can we still be friends?

3. If you really loved your kids, you wouldn't let them eat at McDonald's. If you had kids, you'd understand that your statement is bullshit. Here's the thing, McDonald's is going to happen. It's just too powerful. I hate the place. I hate the food. I hate the way the toys seem to be breeding in my backseat. But kids love going to McDonald's, just like you love going to Starbucks. It's expensive and unhealthy, but sometimes it just makes the day a lot easier.

4. Even with kids keeping a house clean isn't that hard. The secret is to deep clean it once and just maintain it. When you say maintain it, you mean put the kids outside with a water dish and a bowl of food until they're 18, right? Or you mean my wife quitting school and me quitting my two jobs, so we can both stay home and pick up crap, right? What exactly does "maintain it" look like to you? Because I don't want to speak for your children, but mine are little tornados of boogers, poop, and toys. Last week I found two pairs of underwear in my freezer. Between my sofa cushions is Silly Putty. It's been there for more than a year now. Very resilient stain. How does that stuff fit into your advice?

5. Your baby would sleep through the night if you let her cry it out. You may be right, but the thing is, I just can't. I can't be that hard on my baby. I can't stand to do it. So I will suffer the extra few months of sleepless nights until she figures it out. Basically, what I'm saying here is the next time I tell you that I'm tired from being up all night, don't give me advice. Just shut your stupid face and let me bitch.

6. Keeping your children from throwing fits in public begins in the home. I'm going to assume that when you raised children, it was socially okay to beat them. Because here is the thing, I work really hard to teach my kids how to act appropriately in public. But then we get out there, and they turn into screaming, needing, wanting maniacs. It's like showing a werewolf the moon. And honestly, most of the time they are fine. Most of the time they are sweet and wonderful. So please realize that the fit you witnessed is not the norm. But what I can say is taking my kids out into public, telling them no, letting them throw a fit, and then telling them no again, really is the only way they are going to figure out how to be a quiet and reserved person. You know—an understanding person (like the kind of person who doesn't give unsolicited advice in a grocery store).

MY DAUGHTER IS
NOT A PRINCESS

Tristan had soccer practice at the high school. I always brought Norah to practice so she could play with her friend Jill (they went to church together) and a little boy named Jacob, who was the younger brother of one of Tristan's teammates. Jill was a sweet girl with dirty blond hair that spindled down her back and a build similar to Norah's. Jacob, the same age as Norah, had blond hair, blue eyes, and a handsome smile.

A perfect prince.

Both Jill and Norah loved Disney princesses. I doubt that Jacob was into them, but I can say that he seemed to be really into attention, particularly from girls. He followed Norah and Jill around, doing whatever they asked of him.

The three often played a game called The Prince. This game had many variations. Sometimes Norah acted like she was sleeping on the grass. She'd always hold a dandelion against her chest like it was the rose Snow White held after biting the apple. Jill would cry next to Norah, mourning the loss of her dear friend. And then Jacob would creep up, hunch down and kiss Norah on the cheek. Norah would open her eyes, stretch out her arms and sit up. Then she would say something to the tune of, "My prince. You are so wonderful. You saved me."

Sometimes one of the girls was a monster, and it was Jacob's job to fight his way to the princess and save her. And sometimes both girls took turns dancing with Jacob, slowly and gracefully like little Cinderellas at the ball. And when things got really crazy, usually near the end of soccer practice, one of the girls was locked in a tower (an imaginary tower that sat behind a bush near the top of some steps leading to the high school).

There were a few things that bugged me about this game.

First off, Norah was always helpless and waiting for a man to save her. I couldn't understand why she didn't slay the dragon herself. I really like the idea of Norah growing up to be an empowered woman, and I hated seeing her appear so dependent on some heroic male stranger, particularly this little booger eater.

Secondly, I looked at Jacob as he fought past a dragon to win the hand of my daughter, and I pondered on his real intentions. Sure, he seemed heroic. But I hadn't seen his résumé. Perhaps he seemed like a clean-cut hero on the outside but was actually a player. I mean, honestly, how many princesses had he deceived with this dragon slaying bit? Was this a one-time act of valor? Or was it a clever ruse that he used to get into princesses' quarters after hours? Perhaps the dragon was Jacob's wingman, two old barroom buddies pulling a fast one.

I suppose what I am trying to get at is that, as I watched them play, I worried that Norah was developing unrealistic expectations. Would she grow up and look for nothing but the handsome Prince Charming, the perfect man who lived in a castle and rode a noble steed? The prince who was soft but rugged, wealthy but humble, war-hardened but tender, dreamy yet achievable. Would she accept nothing but this contradiction? This unachievable man who would fight a dragon, climb a tower, or set up an elaborate shoe-fitting scheme to find her?

Sometimes I wonder if Disney is teaching Norah to long for a shady character from the streets who impersonates a sultan to win her love (*Aladdin*). Or perhaps an eccentric man who traps her in his castle until she learns to love him (*Beauty and the Beast*). Or maybe the caliber of man that wanders around the forest kissing dead women, hoping to bring them back to life (*Snow White*). All of these characters have labels in the real world: player, stalker, and creeper.

I've never studied Disney. I'm not a scholar in Disney theory (yes, there is such a thing as Disney theory). This is all based on my own observations. And this is not to say that Disney movies don't teach some good morals. But at the same time, they are a cluster of mixed signals and contradictions, many of which make me nervous.

I had a friend after high school. He had dark hair, dark eyes, and olive skin. He came from a wealthy family and he drove an expensive car. He was a really good-looking man, and he came across as charming, humble, and generous. On the surface, he was Prince Charming. But he really had one interest: to get laid. And he did get laid. Often. He was a player in every clichéd sense of the word. He lied. He cheated. He broke a lot of hearts, he took a lot of virtue, and he was proud of it. In my early 20s, I recall being a little jealous of his ability to get women.

He seemed to have some magical power. But now I see guys like that as predators, lurking for girls like my daughter. I've met many of them over the years. There seems to be one in every town I've lived in, every job I've worked, and every university I've attended.

Every time I watch *Cinderella* with Norah, I look at Prince Charming and see my former friend, the player. I wonder what his real intentions are. I wondered if he was only looking to take advantage of Cinderella. I wonder if it was all a ploy, set up to get all the girls in the kingdom to sleep with him.

I suppose this means I'm jaded. Perhaps I am an overprotective father.

The biggest problem is that I'm no Prince Charming. I mean, I'm a nice guy. I love my wife and my kids. I try really hard to be a good father and husband. But here are the facts: I'm not tall, dark, and handsome, and I don't make much money. I am a stocky 5'11." I work in education. I have a white-collar education but earn a blue-collar wage. I don't own a castle or a carriage but rather a 1,100-square-foot home and a 13-year-old S-10 pickup with a dented bumper. I've never been to a formal ball or even a formal dinner. I don't know how to dance. When I think of a nice meal, I think of the Olive Garden. I've worn a tux three times in my life—at my brother's wedding, my sister's wedding, and my own. I hated every moment of it.

Perhaps it's jealousy. Perhaps I've always wanted to be Prince Charming.

I don't know, but what I do know is that I want the best for Norah. I don't want her to become a princess. I want her to grow up to be a well-rounded woman who values people for their qualities, not their possessions. I don't want her to be looking for some man that doesn't exist and wind up finding some user, some player posing to be a prince. And yet, I want her to find someone better than myself. Someone a little better looking, who is sweeter and more understanding. I want her to be able to spot the real Prince Charming. And I want her to be able to spot a player. I want her to love someone not because they own a castle or a nice horse, but because they are a good person with values and virtues. Someone who will not treat her like a princess, but treat her like a partner.

THE COPYCAT GAME IS FOR A-HOLES

Tristan and I stood in the kitchen. It was evening, and Tristan was in his Spiderman pajamas. It was just the two of us having a late dinner. I handed him some chicken nuggets, and then I asked, "You want some tater tots?"

Tristan looked up at me, eyes blue and excited, and said, "You want some tater tots?"

I will admit I was confused at first. I was 20 years rusty when it came to the copycat game. And I suppose the most infuriating thing about playing the copycat game is that no one says, "Hey, want to play copycat?" Because if they did, the person would probably just reply by saying, "Hey, want to play copycat?" Then there would be confusion and eventual frustration. But ultimately that is the point of playing copycat, right? To get someone really aggravated by repeating everything they say.

It's really a game for assholes.

"No," I said. "I don't want any tater tots. I was asking you if you wanted some tater tots."

Tristan smiled, like he had me.

He'd obviously learned this from one of our neighbor kids, who are mostly assholes. I know this because they regularly eat my food without asking, pee on my toilet seat, peek in my windows, and tell me I have a messy house. For some reason this kind of crap is acceptable from children. I'm supposed to write it off as them learning how to be adults. However, if an adult did all of those things at my house, I'd probably kick their ass. But because they are children, I have to be understanding.

I love my children, but their friends are shitheads.

"No," Tristan said with a fat grin. "I don't want any tater tots. I was asking you if you wanted some tater tots."

It was then that I realized what he was up to. I didn't speak for a moment. I chose my words carefully. I thought about my education, my graduate degrees. I thought about the fact that I worked at a university and taught college classes. Then I thought about my age and life wisdom. I thought about the fact that Tristan was a seven-year-old.

I got this, I thought. *I can win this game. And while I'm at it, I'll teach him a valuable lesson about respecting his father. I'm going to bring this kid down.*

Because the fact is, I invented the copycat game. I was a regional champion back in the day. I knew all about what it meant to make someone so irritated by repeating what they said that they turned red-faced and angry and ended up driving their car off a cliff.

Ok, no one ever committed suicide based on my ability to annoy them—though I'm certain they contemplated it. Particularly schoolteachers. And my siblings.

Although I was rusty, I felt confident that I could still show my seven-year-old son who was the master.

"My name is Tristan Flip Edwards, and I smell like Hot. Steaming. Farts." I looked down at Tristan with a large smile that seemed to say, *Put that in your rainbow and see if it shines. You don't come into my neighborhood without game.*

Tristan fell right into my trap and repeated my phrase. I responded with, "Oh! So you admit that you smell like hot, steaming farts!"

Tristan thought about it for a moment. He looked down at the floor; his right heel bounced up and down a few times. Clearly I'd shown him a very valuable life lesson: don't f@#% with Dad.

Then he looked up at me, gave me a shit-eating grin, and said, "Oh! So you admit that you smell like hot, steaming farts!"

Then he laughed, long and hard, right in my face.

Damn! I thought. *Now I was the one who smelled like a fart.*

I admit, I got frustrated. I honestly thought that would work. I looked at my son staring up at me, trying hard to keep his game face but letting small giggles slip out, and I realized that I might be in over my head. I tried a few more tricks. A few more ways to turn things around on him, but none of them got him to stop repeating everything I said. Rather, they resulted in me admitting that I ate poo or smelled like garbage or wore bacon as underwear. I tried to remind myself that this game was ridiculous and asinine, and it didn't matter. But the fact was Tristan was a seven-year-old, and he was getting me to admit to all kinds of things I didn't want to. He was driving me nuts, and dinner was getting cold.

There is something really depressing about losing to a seven-year-old, even if it is a stupid game. I know that there are fathers out there who would see something like this as a source of pride, like when your child finishes college when you never graduated. But that wasn't the case. I was too prideful. I felt like a failure. I was an educated adult, and I should be able to outsmart my son. But I couldn't.

I told him to stop, and he repeated it. I told him about the cold dinner and that it was after bedtime, he repeated that too.

I realized that going at this situation in the traditional fashion was not going work. So I broke the rules.

Our meal was Tristan's favorite—dinosaur-shaped chicken nuggets from the frozen section and tater tots.

His blue spaceship plate was sitting on the counter, stocked with his favorite food.

"You can eat my dinner," I said.

Without thinking about it, Tristan repeated what I said.

So I reached out and started eating.

"Oh man! These are some good chicken nuggets."

Tristan reached up. He told me to stop. He reminded me that those were his chicken nuggets.

"You going to stop repeating everything I say?" I said.

Tristan thought about it for a bit. He reached up and tried to steal the plate, but I held it out of his reach. Finally, he agreed.

I didn't eat all of his dinner. Just one nugget, but it was enough to get him to stop.

So often with parenting, I have to stoop down to the level of a child. I have to try to get my son to admit that he smells like a fart to get him to stop doing something childish or reach out and steal some of his dinner. It is in moments like these I realize that I obviously haven't matured much past that of a little boy. Regardless of my age and education, I sometimes feel like a child raising a child.

I replaced the nugget I ate off Tristan's plate with one of mine. As I did, he looked up at me with misty eyes. He was about to cry. I gave him his food, put my arm around him, and said, "Tristan. You totally won that game of copycat. You beat me so bad that the only way I could get you back was to steal your dinner. You are the copycat master."

Tristan smiled at me. Then he let out a long, sinister laugh.

Later Mel came home to father and son sitting together on the sofa watching Teenage Mutant Ninja Turtles while we ate our nuggets.

"How'd things go?" she asked.

"How'd things go?" Tristan and I both said.

Mel rolled her eyes.

Tristan and I laughed.

CRAZY THINGS SAID WHEN UP WITH KIDS

There is something crazed and stressful about getting up in the night with children, and Mel and I tend to say angry, spiteful, and sometimes crazy things when sleep deprived. Both of us realize that what we are saying is drafted somewhere between dream and reality and not representative of our regular feelings towards each other or the kids. Therefore, we decided early in our marriage to not hold grudges because of what was said in the night. Below are a few examples.

"It's your turn. I was just up for an hour listening to Norah cry and your stupid snoring. You sound like you're dying."

"If you slam one more door, I'm going to take all the doors off the hinges and shove them up your butt."

"Turn off the bathroom light! You don't need light to pee! I pee in the dark all the time."

"I left Norah's wet pull-up in her bed. Or maybe I put it in the laundry. I don't know… I'm too tired. Will you figure it out?"

"I don't know where Bun-Bun is and I don't care. Go to sleep. I've been up for over an hour with you. If you don't go to sleep, I'm going to find Bun-Bun and light him on fire."

"I don't know if there's a trailer or something, but the pee is everywhere."

"He won't sleep because his bum burns. It's probably because of his diaper rash. Can we just pack it with ice or something?"

"Tristan, I love you, but if you don't go to sleep, I might die. Is that what you want? For me to die because I feel like I'm dying. Do you even care?"

"Stop screaming! It's making my head explode."

"Thanks for getting up with her. It makes me want you. I'm too tired, but I wanted you to know about it."

"Stop asking me for Reese's Pieces. It's 4 a.m.! I'm going to eat them all! Right in front of you. And you will have none, and I will have a tummy ache. I hate everything right now."

"The baby just pooped on my hand and you have gas! It smells like death. I swear, if you fart one more time, I'm going to kill you."

"Tristan wet the bed. I took off his pants and put down some towels. It's cool."

"Listen, I know that your tummy hurts. I get that. But you need to puke in the bowl, OK? It's not that hard. Just stick your stupid face in there and let out your stupid puke into the stupid bowl!"

"I don't know what's going on. Norah is a kitty and looking for tickle spiders and it smells like old people."

"Why am I crying?! Because every time I fall asleep the baby cries, you kick me, or Norah asks for a blanket. Every time! This is why parents drive into the ocean."

"Sometimes when I'm up with the kids like this, it feels like I'm in a dark hole."

"You are old enough to get your own drink of water. What you are scared of in the kitchen isn't half as frightening as what I'm about to become."

"How are you sleeping through this? Is sleep your mutant power?"

"If you go to sleep right now, I'll give you a whole box of cookies for breakfast."

MY FIRST EVENING ALONE WITH THREE KIDS (A TRIP THROUGH HELL)

We'd just had a baby, and I was home alone for the first time with three kids. I was in the kitchen, packing my lunch for the next day, feeling confident.

Mel was out signing up our daughter for soccer. My mother-in-law left two days earlier. Tristan had come home from school early because he had a fever. He was sacked out on the sofa. Norah had wrapped herself in a bath towel and was telling me that she was the fairy princess.

It was adorable.

I'd heard so many parents complain about the transition from two kids to three kids. "It's a real game changer. They outnumber you," was the biggest complaint. They spoke like co-captains on a boat. Having one extra crewmember turned the numbers and suddenly, mutiny took place, and they lost command.

I thought about our ship, how two of the crewmembers were sleeping and one was being cute, and wondered what was wrong with these other parents. This wasn't so bad. In fact, it was enjoyable.

What a bunch of pansies other parents are.

"You are the fairy king," Norah said, bowing.

Yes, I thought. *I'm the king.*

She asked if I wanted to see her fly.

"Sure."

Norah ran into the living room, the towel on her arms spread wide like wings, and ran right into the bouncer. She didn't crash into it or anything—more of just a hard bump that was strong enough to wake the baby—and set in motion a trip through hell.

Aspen started crying, which woke Tristan. Now that he was awake, he remembered that he was sick. He started moaning long dramatic cries. Then he ran into the bathroom and puked. Half of it got into the bowl; the other half ran down his shirt.

He sniffled and gagged with big, boogery cries.

I was holding the baby in my right arm and rubbing Tristan's back with the left. I stood awkwardly, leaning to the right, trying to keep Aspen away from Tristan so she wouldn't get sick. She was still crying, then she stopped for a moment, and I noticed that she was trying to latch onto my bicep.

For the first time in my life, I longed to have breasts.

Breastfeeding makes me feel completely helpless. Mel bottle-fed our other two kids, and although she saw this as a mark of failure (she tried to breastfeed, but things kept getting in the way), I, at least, had more control over the situation. I could feed the baby. But right then, as Aspen rooted around for a nipple, I was 100 percent useless.

Tristan started gagging once again, and so did I from the smell of his puke. Then Norah, the fairy princess started tugging at the baby and saying, "What's wrong baby? What's wrong? Do you want me to kiss you?"

Norah really loves the baby. It's cute and wonderful that she wants to be a big helper. But honestly, in that moment, it was a huge pain in the ass. I was trying to comfort Tristan and the baby, while doing my best not to puke, and suddenly Norah was yanking at my arm, about to flip me over, so she could ram her face into Aspen's, pinch her cheeks, kiss her forehead, and say, "Don't cry little baby. Don't cry."

Norah thinks *this* is parenting. She thinks this will help, when the last thing Aspen wants is another kid getting all kissy with her. What she wanted was milk, from a boob, but no one in the house had them.

I snapped.

"Norah," I said. "You're not helping. Ok. Just leave the baby alone. Go watch a show on the iPad or something. I don't want you getting sick, and you're just making the baby angry."

She looked up at me with big, soggy eyes, the towel still wrapped around her arms like wings. "I'm never ever talking to you ever again!"

Then she went into her room and started crying.

All three kids were crying now.

One needed food that I couldn't give her. One was covered in vomit and needed me to help change him. And the other needed comfort. All of them wanted me right then, and all I could think about was the fact that I was now in hell. I knew that just one month ago, before we had Aspen, I could've easily handled this situation. But now, trying to hold a crying baby while caring for a puking kid and an emotionally distraught little girl, felt like too much.

Having two kids felt like a picnic on the beach. Having three kids felt like drowning.

I coached Tristan out of his puke soaked clothes and into his pajamas. Got him into bed with a puke bowl. Once I finished with him, Mel was back. She took Aspen into the living room to feed her.

I went into Norah's room. She had her face buried into her pillow, hands over the back of her head.

I told her I was sorry, and she said, "Go away, Daddy."

"That's too bad," I said. "As the fairy king, I really wanted to see you fly again. Perhaps I could even help."

She looked up at me and tried not to smile, but I could see it creeping into the side of her face.

"Do you want to fly like a fairy?" I asked.

She stood up, put the towel on her arms, and I lifted her up and carried her around the house for a while. Suddenly we were good again. I got her into bed and the house was quiet.

I sat down next to Mel. She was still feeding Aspen. I told her what happened while she was away.

"I don't ever want to be alone with all three of them ever again," I said. "That was hell. Why did we have a third child?"

"What are you complaining about?" Mel asked. "I'm going to be alone with them every day."

I looked at her in the eyes and asked, "How are you going to keep from going crazy?"

At the time, it all seemed hopeless. As a parent, I had no idea how I was ever going to make three kids work. But at the same time, I hadn't known how I was ever going to make one kid work—or two. It's the transition—the addition of a new child—that is the hardest, not the number.

Mel let out a breath. "It will get better," she said. "I'm sure."

"Yes," I said. "Let's think happy thoughts."

HELL IS A LOT LIKE A LITTLE GIRL'S BIRTHDAY PARTY

I was in my backyard with about ten little girls between the ages of three and eight. It was a hot day in Small Town, Oregon, close to 100 degrees, unusual weather for this part of the country. Norah was turning five, and this was her birthday party.

I assume hell is a lot like a little girl's birthday party.

The party guests sat in a circle. Most wore dresses. All had tiaras. Norah was wearing a long blond wig that she said made her look "like a glamour princess."

All sat on folding chairs beneath my porch awning. We played a game with similar rules to musical chairs, only the girls didn't get up while the music was going. Instead, they passed around a bottle of nail polish. I controlled the music, only I didn't really understand the game. I didn't understand why painting nails was such a big deal. I feel like Norah is in such a hurry to grow up. She wants to get her ears pierced. She wants to start dating boys. She wants to do her own hair. She wants to be more than five, yet I want her to be sweet and little forever.

I stopped the music, and whoever was holding the bottle got to paint one nail. The winner of the game was going to have all their nails painted. I didn't know this part. I thought the game stopped once everyone had at least one nail painted. I drew this conclusion because each time I stopped the music, every little girl that didn't have at least one painted nail flipped their shit. "Oh! This game is unfair." Or, "I never win anything." Or, "I hate her!"

I'd never seen anything quite like this mix of rage and sorrow.

I started to time the music so each girl would have at least one painted nail because I am a fair and reasonable guy—and, also, because it seemed like the best way to stop the screaming. Eventually, Mel gave me a funny look, told me how the game was won, and asked why I was making it take so long. By then each girl had at least one nail painted, and as Mel and I spoke, several girls ran off into the yard, their arms in the air like fleeing prisoners.

The whole party was like this—a struggle to keep the attention of these little girls so they wouldn't either run into the yard and pull plants out of the garden or run into the house and play with the toilet. A friend of mine used to work at a drug and alcohol rehab clinic, and I couldn't help but think of some of the stories he told me of managing drug addicts as I watched Mel wrangle the girls from the yard and back under the porch, while the ones still in the chairs looked at their one painted nail, faces a mix of sorrow and frustration because they hadn't won the game.

Three parents attended the party—Mel, Mel's friend Emilie, and myself. We were outnumbered, and the children knew it. Sometimes they split up, with one group running off into the yard while the other ran into the house. Sometimes they worked in a large group, crowding around the birthday cake and using their mighty numbers to overshadow their little fingers clawing at the frosting.

Eventually we gave up on the nail painting game and moved on to opening presents.

The little girls sat in the circle again, each one of them looking at Norah. Every gift was in pink and purple wrapping paper. All gifts were either Disney Princess-themed or soft and cuddly with big lovable eyes. With the opening of each gift, Norah held it over her head for all to see. Every time, the girls responded with loud, terrifying screeching sounds that made the neighbor's dog bark.

Once the cake was served and the children finished eating, I turned my back to set up the princess piñata. When I turned around, the little creatures had striped the reminder of Norah's birthday cake of frosting, leaving little more than drool dripping from the corners.

The piñata was supposed to look like Belle from *Beauty and the Beast*. But to me it just looked like a woman in a yellow dress hanging from a rope attached to the top of her scalp. I know that we bought this piñata with the best of intentions, but frankly we were going to hang a representation of a woman by a rope from the rafters of my patio, then beat it with a stick until its insides fell out. It was disturbing. When I asked Norah earlier that day if she really wanted to beat up on Belle, she replied, "She's a bad princess."

"Really? Is that what you do to bad princesses? Beat them with a stick?"

Norah looked up at me with soft blue green eyes. "Yup!"

I honestly felt that using the princess piñata was a little morbid, but I didn't want to be a party pooper, so I just hung the damn thing.

We went from youngest to oldest. The first little girl, Anca, was about four years old. She approached the piñata nervously, not sure what she was going to do, but after the first swing, I could only describe the look in her eyes as blood lust. She then started beating the hell out of it, and eventually we had to pull her back and give another girl a try. Each girl looked at the princess dangling there. They didn't think about the fact that this looked like a real person; instead, they thought about candy and destruction.

Cassandra, one of the older girls at about seven, managed to knock off the princess's head. Still, the candy didn't come out, so

I had to wrap a rope around her torso and string her up again. Now we had a headless princess hanging in our yard with little girls screaming and beating it with a stick.

The whole event was not a shining moment for me as a father. Frankly, it's something I'd like to put behind me.

At one point, my son Tristan grabbed the princess's head and began beating it against the side of the house and laughing. I asked him why he would do that. His response was, "I thought there was candy inside."

"No," I said. "There isn't. The candy is in the..." I wanted to say headless princess, but stopped short, and simply demanded that he give me the severed head. When he refused, I had to wrestle it out of his hands.

Eventually a little girl busted open what was left of the princess, and the torso fell to the ground, spilling its insides. The children rushed at the candy, kicking the wounded, headless princess to the side. Due to the heat, the chocolate inside had started melting. Once they collected the candy, I looked around at the children circling the headless body. Their hands and faces were covered in chocolate. They looked like feasting animals, paws and jaws covered in rich, dark fluid.

It was terrifying.

But what scared me even worse was when I looked at the clock. The party was supposed to end at four, but it was only 3:40. This meant that we'd run out of activities, and we still had a good 20 minutes before parents came to pick up their kids. And if these parents were anything like me, they surely would be late.

I mean, I love my kids. But I also savor the moments that I can spend alone with my wife, and being 10 or 15 minutes late to pick up the kids is excusable for most people, and it means 10 or 15 glorious minutes of just Mel and myself. I assume a lot of parents think this way. But usually, showing up late to pick up your kids means leaving the caregiver with just one or two extra kids at the house. Not nine extra kids full of blood lust and chocolate. Long story short, I knew that it would be a good half hour to 45 minutes before I got all these munchkins out of the house, and we had no more activities in our back pockets.

I looked at Mel. "What are we going to do?"

Mel looked at me with a little fear in her eyes. "I don't know..."

I thought about letting them finish coloring the pictures they started at the beginning of the party, but I soon realized that all the crayons had melted in the sun. The girls started wandering into the house, which I didn't want, so we let them into the yard and hoped that they didn't destroy our garden. Basically, I closed my eyes and prayed for the best. It wasn't until later that I realized the little terrors pulled up three tomato plants and placed a Barbie head on a stick next to the bird bath in what I assumed was some *Lord of the Flies* expression of dominance.

Thinking back, I probably should've just started a game of tag or red light/green light. But by this point I was good and tired and not thinking at my regular capacity.

Eventually, parents arrived. Many of them late, like I suspected.

Once the party was over, I started cleaning up. In my yard, I found candy wrappers, the severed head of a princess piñata, chewed gum, melted chocolate, cake frosting, a new colony of ants, the piñata torso, a scabby Disney Princess Band-Aid, rocks, an ownerless shoe, popped balloons, melted candles, four tiaras, three princess goody bags, and two boogers next to the stripped cake.

Once I got things cleaned up, I plopped down in the living room. Norah was playing with one of her new toys, and she climbed into my lap to show it to me. She was in a white dress that was spackled with chocolate, frosting, and crayon.

"That is really cute," I said. "Did you have fun at your party?"

Norah looked at me with a big smile and nodded her head, excitedly. Although she didn't say anything, I knew that this was a good memory that she would hold onto for some time.

"Good," I said. "I love you, little person."

THINGS I'D LOVE TO DO TO MY CHILDREN ONCE THEY ARE ADULTS

When I was in my late teens, my mother would always tell me she planned to come to my adult home, turn my ceiling fan on high, and throw toys into it, just like I'd done when I was a kid. She had a lot of these statements, and I always thought she was being ridiculous—until I had children of my own.

Below is my list of things I'd love to do to my children once they are adults, so they will understand how tolerant I was as a parent.

1. Hide in my daughter's pantry and crap my pants. (I hear this is a perk of old age.)
2. Punch my son in the balls while shopping at Target. Then laugh in his face.
3. Knock on my son's door moments before he is about to have sex and insist that he get me a glass of water.
4. Loudly argue with my son while grocery shopping about whether or not he can smell my fart.

5. Sit on my daughter's lap while at church and wet my pants. Then loudly deny everything.
6. While my daughter's living room is full of guests, walk out naked and then act offended when I'm asked to get dressed.
7. Poop in the tub and ask them to fish it out (this applies to all my children).
8. Urinate on a tree in my son's backyard while he is hosting a family reunion BBQ.
9. Push on my son's early-30s gut and ask, "Are you having a baby?" Preferably while his wife and friends are around.
10. Write "BOOGER" in marker on the backseat of my son's car.

WHAT I DON'T UNDERSTAND ABOUT MY KIDS

I came into having kids with this stupid assumption: I was once a kid, so I should know all about them. But over the years, I've learned that kids are mysterious little creatures. Every day they confuse the hell out of me. Here are a few reasons why.

They can so quickly forgive: A few years ago, Tristan's friend punched him in the face before stealing his string cheese. About fifteen minutes later, they played in the living room as if nothing happened. If a friend of mine punched me in the face and stole my string cheese, I'd need at least a year and probably a legal settlement to get over it. (And I'm not even that big a fan of string cheese.)

Be completely comfortable after peeing their pants: There are times when Norah has peed her pants and it has gone unnoticed for an hour or more. Mostly because she just doesn't care. Neither the smell nor the wet feeling changes her mood. Once it dries and gets itchy, well, that doesn't faze her either. She simply plays it off with a cool, collective face that seems to say, *Nothing wrong here.*

How they can be 100% shameless: Both my kids have strutted out into the front yard naked during high noon, and they have dropped their pants in front of guests. Mel and I have had many discussions with them about decency, but it doesn't seem to matter. If they are tired of itchy pants and a cramped shirt, they come off.

How they can eat boogers: Sadly, I don't think this requires much explanation. Just yuck!

How they can block out everything but the TV: If a show is on that they really enjoy, they exhibit a concentration that is worthy of Albert Einstein. They can tune out almost anything—my voice, fire engines, a nuclear blast. One time I tried to get Tristan's attention while he was watching Pokémon. I yelled, snapped my fingers, and clapped. I even banged a pot with a wooden spoon. Nothing worked. Eventually, I shut off the TV and he nearly shit himself.

Why they always choose Mom over me: It doesn't matter what I bribe them with, how much fun we had together that day, if I've been their primary caregiver for the past several months, or if I am the closest person to the accident. If Mom is within view, she is always picked over me. I try not to take this personally because, let's face it, my wife is amazing. But I cannot help but feel a little jealous when Norah is hurt and, when I try to help her, she puts her hand on my face, pushes me away, and cries for Mommy.

How they can so easily warm my heart: I know this sounds cheesy, but there is something about the simple phrase, "I love you, Daddy," that wins me over every time. For example: once Norah drew on the only nice chair we have in our living room with permanent red marker. I was flaming pissed. But when I confronted her about it, she looked up at me with big blue eyes and said, "I'm *sowry*, Daddy," in a voice that was a mix between Minnie Mouse and a songbird. A switch flipped inside me from rage to tenderness, and all I wanted to do was give her a hug. I call this ability to change my mood Norah's Cute Powers, and I wonder if God gave children the ability to melt their parents' hearts to keep us from killing them.

WHODUNIT? (THE INTERROGATION)

The restroom smelled of urine. I could see yellow around the toilet bolts, along the side of the bowl, and slowing drying in a pool on the tile.

We have two bathrooms. One for the kids and one for the adults.

I was in the kids' bathroom.

I knew someone was going to have to clean it up, and I didn't want it to be Mel or me. Me for obvious reasons. And Mel because I'd have to hear about it.

So much of parenting comes down to solving a *whodunit* mystery. Confessions are difficult and evidence is everywhere.

My first suspect was Tristan (my seven-year-old). Norah, our-four-year, was not built to do this kind of damage. Nor was Mel. So this meant it was down to the boy or me.

I found him in the kitchen, eating Lucky Charms and playing on the iPad.

"Dude. Did you pee all over the toilet?"

His eyes opened wide and his jaw went slack. He gave me a look of innocence, one that seemed to say, "Don't hurt me."

I've never hit my son. Or any of my kids. I have no intentions of ever doing so. But when he's in trouble, he always looks at me like I might, at any time, snap and lay into him like a schoolteacher from the 40s. I will be the first to admit that I love this power. I'm sure that, at some later age, he will not fear me anymore. He will see me as just some old man, weak and feeble and unable to enforce anything. But right now, with Tristan being seven, I feel all-powerful. I am alpha. I am omega.

I am the giver.

I am the punisher.

"No! I didn't pee all over the place," Tristan said.

He was nervous. He was trembling. He was suspicious. He started to speak in nonsense. "I don't...even pee. I mean...I haven't peed today. It was probably Norah."

"Really, Tristan? All day?" I started interrogating. "It's 2 p.m. And Norah isn't equipped to do that kind of damage...unless she peed in a cup and poured it all over the place."

I looked at Norah. She was sitting in the living room watching *Word Girl*. She smiled back at me, and I was struck with fear that I'd given her an idea.

Tristan and I went back and forth for a while, but he was quickly running out of explanations. He tried blaming it on his mother. He tried blaming it on me. I'm sure he'd blame the dog if we had one. Eventually he said, "It was Taran!"

Taran was the neighbor boy who spent most of his free time at our house. And indeed, he sat in our living room earlier that morning. I thought I had Tristan pinned until that moment.

This Taran explanation really spoiled my interrogation. Thinking back, I am proud of his ability to find an alternative. It showed his unwillingness to back down, but at the time, I was angry because I had thought I had him!

"You know what, it was either you or Taran," I said. "Taran is your friend. That means his pee is your responsibility. Get in there and clean it up."

Tristan gave me a terrified look because he knew I had him!

"I can't clean it up," he said. "I don't know how."

"I'm NOT cleaning up your friend's pee," I said.

I set him up with a toilet brush and some cleaner. I told him what to do. He was scrubbing away, his eyes a little misty, when Mel came home from the store.

I told her what happened. I told her about the interrogation. How I'd nailed Tristan! And now he was cleaning the toilet.

I smiled with satisfaction.

"Little boys are so gross," I said. "I'm not going to clean up his messes. He needs to learn that."

I assumed she'd be proud of me.

Mel gave me a curt smile, and then she asked me to follow her into our restroom. I asked her why, but she didn't respond.

Once next to the toilet, she pointed at the floor near the front of the bowl. There was a small pool of pee.

I got nervous.

"Every morning it's there. Every. Morning. It's the reason I put slippers on when I get up in the night. I can't count how many times I've stepped in YOUR PEE in the middle of the night and had to change my socks and clean my feet. Then I end up cleaning YOUR mess. You are just as gross as he is. Only you're 31 and he's seven."

I wanted to stand up for myself. I wanted to blame Tristan. If we had a dog, I'd have thought about blaming it. I wanted to tell her that I don't turn on the light in the night so that I won't wake her, and that's why I can't hit the bowl. But really, I'm just lazy. I wanted to tell her that I'd never do it again, but I didn't know if I could commit to that. So I didn't say anything.

I was busted.

Mel left the room, and as she walked down the hall, she stopped at the kids' bathroom and said, "Tristan, thanks for cleaning the toilet. Once you are done with the toilet brush, give it to your father. He needs to clean the pee he got on our toilet."

I listened to Tristan laugh—and felt like an ass.

THE DAY MOM TOOK
AWAY THE TOYS

It was Tuesday, around 7:30 p.m., and Mel and Norah were arguing. I was in the kitchen grading papers for my second job, and Mel was trying to get the kids to clean up and get ready for bed before their 8 o'clock bedtime. Tristan was cleaning in his room. Norah, dressed in ballerina pajamas, her hair wet and combed, stood in the hallway, her arms folded in protest.

Usually this is my job.

Generally, I come home from work, have dinner with the family, and then get the kids to bed while Mel does homework. But Tuesdays were different because that's when papers were due in the online classes I taught.

And I must admit that it makes me feel a little better about my role as a father to hear Mel struggle to get the kids to listen as much as I do. After all, she's the popular one.

Just a few days ago, Tristan received enough chore points to go out for ice cream. I asked him who he wanted to go with. Without hesitation, he said, "Mom."

"You know," I said. "I'll let you get more ice cream and toppings. The cone will be as big as your head. I will let you pick the radio station. I might even slip you $100."

He stuck out his lip and said, "Mom."

Sure, the $100 was an exaggeration. But even if it were real, I don't think he'd have changed his mind.

This same scene played out a million times with both kids. They always want to sit next to Mom at dinner or while watching a movie. Sometimes Norah will, without reason, say, "I only love mommy!"

"But I love you, too," I say.

Norah usually stomps her foot and yells, "Only mommy!"

I try not to take stuff like this personally, but it's frustrating as hell. I want to be the popular one. I want the kids to fight over me. I want to go out for ice cream.

Sometimes I wonder if the reason my kids like Mel more than me is because of my nightly duty of getting them to clean up the living room and get ready for bed. On workdays, I really only get about 1 to 2 hours a day with my kids. And half of that time is spent with me yelling things like, "Stop screwing around," "It's not time to eat cheese! It's time to pick up your crap," "WTF kids?" (I'm not looking forward to the day I have to explain what that means), and "Do you realize how fast this would go if you'd just do it! I wouldn't have to yell if you'd listen to me." Most days, I feel like all my kids hear is my angry voice.

While In contrast, Mel gets to have a healthy mix of angry, frustrated mom moments and loving, fun, compassionate moments. I really only get that mix of emotions on weekends. One of the first things I learned about working one-on-one with students is that sometimes you have to tear them down a little bit when they aren't performing the way you want them to. But you have to be sure to build them back up before they leave or they will never come back. The same method seems to apply to my kids. During the week I only have time to tear them down because they aren't getting their chores done. And by the time everything is said and done, and they are in bed, we are all too tired to build anything, particularly emotions. Then there's only so much time on the weekends to build them back up.

That night Mel was having a difficult time getting Norah to listen. Her room, like usual, was an explosion of baby dolls wrapped in blankets. I'm not sure the exact number of dolls Norah has, but it I think it's somewhere between a million and infinity. And it's not always dolls that she's caring for. Her maternal instincts reach out to stuffed animals, remote controls, shoe boxes…really anything that can be wrapped in a blanket. Just last week I found her swaddling one of my work shoes in a Hello Kitty blanket, cooing, "You're just such a cutie! Now go to sleep."

I watched Mel from the hallway. She kept telling Norah to put the babies away, and Norah kept stomping her foot and yelling, "Shhhhhhh!!! The babies are sleeping!"

It was close to 8 now. The two had argued for nearly 20 minutes. Every time Mel went into Norah's room to try to clean things up, Norah started screaming like a protective mother fighting off a kidnapper. "Leave my babies alone!"

Both stood in the hallway now. Mel folded her arms. She'd clearly had it, and I was starting to get frustrated, too. All the yelling was making it difficult to concentrate.

Finally Mel yelled, "You know what. I am giving you until the count of five to start cleaning. And if you don't, I'm putting all of your toys in boxes. Every one of them. All your babies! Your Legos! Your princess dresses! Everything!" I often describe Mel as a soft-spoken introvert, so whenever she yells it's really terrifying. Her yelling voice is rather deep and scratchy, reminding me of the possessed girl in *The Exorcist*.

I use the "I'm going to count to 5 tactic" all the time, and it has about a 50% chance of working. Only the consequence is always going to bed early and no bedtime story. I'd never gone as far as to say, "I'm going to take away all your toys."

It seemed extreme.

I leaned back from my laptop to see how this would play out. I assumed that Norah would get busy, but before Mel had the opportunity to start counting, Norah said, "I don't care," in a bratty little voice, her head cocked to the side. Her voice was entitled and irritating. It made me cheer for Mel.

"I'll just get more toys," Norah said.

Mel didn't argue. She didn't count. She didn't say a word. She simply walked with heavy angry steps into the garage. We'd just moved, so we still had a surplus of boxes. Mel came into the house with three large boxes and started packing up Norah's toys.

I assumed that Norah would step in, throw a fit, freak out—something. But she didn't. She just sat on the sofa in the living room and watched. Her face was soft and calm, and I couldn't tell if she really thought that we would buy her all new toys, which we wouldn't, or if she was relieved because the burden of ownership was removed.

I walked down the hall and stood in Norah's doorway.

"Do you really think this is a good idea?" I asked. "It seems a bit extreme."

Mel put the final baby doll in a box full of baby dolls. She looked up at me as she taped it shut.

"I'm sick of this crap. She needs to learn."

"Are you ever going to give them back?" I asked.

She didn't answer my question. She pushed the box towards me and said, "Take this to the garage."

As I hauled the box down the hall through the kitchen, all I could wonder was how this was all going to play out. What were the next few days going to be like? And then I had a selfish thought—perhaps this will make me Norah's favorite.

Around noon the next day, I sent Mel a text: *How's Norah doing without toys? Does she hate you?*

I was hopeful when I sent the text.

Mel replied. *She's doing just fine. In fact, she hasn't had one fit this morning.*

I will admit, I was a little surprised by this response. It was my assumption that Norah, my sweet little Norah, was going to wake up, stretch her little arms above her head, look around her room, realize that all her babies were gone, and flip her shit. In my mind, I saw her sprawled out on the floor, like I'd seen her do a million times, screaming and kicking and crying. I assumed that I'd get a text from Mel sometime in the mid-morning telling me she was ready to commit murder.

But I got none of that.

It had to be just a matter of time, I thought. Perhaps sometime in the mid-afternoon I would find out that Norah cracked, which caused Mel to crack. I had it all planned out. I would come home from work to find Norah freaking out in her room, screaming about how much she hated her mother. Mel would be in the kitchen, ready to pull her hair out. And I would walk into the garage, grab Norah's boxes of toys, and solve the problem in a Jolly Old Saint Nick sort of way.

And once Norah saw that I was the one who brought back her babies, she would wrap her arms around me, lay a huge kiss on my cheek, and say, "I only love Daddy."

Finally, I would be her favorite.

I came home and the living room was the cleanest I'd ever seen it in months. The sofa wasn't lined with swaddled baby dolls like some low-budget foster home. There weren't four or five princess dresses lying on the floor. And Norah bounced around in a great mood.

She ran to the door, gave me a big hug, and said, "I love you, Daddy." Then she waltzed into the living room and danced while humming music.

I looked at Mel with confusion.

"She's been like this all day," Mel said. "It's the craziest thing. It makes me wish I'd taken her toys away a long time ago."

"Are you sure she doesn't hate you?" I asked.

Mel shrugged. "I almost get the impression that she loves me more. She's been really snuggly today, and she keeps telling me that I'm a good mommy."

"Perhaps she's delusional with grief." I said.

"I can live with that if it means she's not screaming."

Later that night, when getting Norah ready for bed, I asked her to brush her teeth.

"No. I don't have to brush my teeth."

We started arguing. I had to chase her down the hall a few times. This was all standard. But what was unusual was after I caught up with her and forced the toothbrush into her hand, she said, "You're just a mean daddy. I only love Mommy!"

I said, "Really, Norah? I'm not the one who took all your toys away."

She sat silent for a moment. She looked me in the face for some time; obviously, she was deep in thought. I assumed that I'd gotten to her. That she was starting to realize that I was, indeed, the cool parent. The better parent.

At least equal to, or maybe even better than, mommy.

I may have just become the favorite.

Instead Norah looked me in the face and cried, "Mommy! I only love Mommy! You're a mean daddy."

Mel could do anything to Norah and she'd still love her more than me. She could lock Norah in the attic and feed her buckets of fish heads, and she'd probably still draw pictures of Mel and her holding hands at the park.

In moments like this, I wonder what I've done to deserve this. Am I really that mean of a dad? Each night I read Norah a story. I get up with her in the night. I take her out on daddy-daughter dates. I let her comb my hair, as painful as that can be. I tell her that I love her every day. And even though I really wanted to put her up on Amazon after she kicked me in the crotch because I made her strap her own shoes, I only put her in her room for ten minutes.

Perhaps I'm a pushover. Maybe I need to be meaner and take things away like Mel did? Perhaps I need to be a jackass of a dad so she will feel like she needs to earn my love. But I'm not that kind of guy, and I don't think I can force myself to be. It's all very frustrating.

A few moments later Mel walked by. "Norah, please do what Daddy says."

She looked up at her mother, then at me, and then placed the toothbrush in her mouth.

We didn't give Norah her toys back for about three weeks. Mostly because she was so well behaved without them that we often forgot we'd taken them away. She never once asked to have them back.

During those three weeks, Norah didn't hold any resentment against her mother. And she still, like always, loved her more than me.

One day I came home from work, and the living room was filled with swaddled babies again. I asked Mel why she gave them back, and she said, "I was starting to feel guilty. Norah's been really sweet the past few weeks. She'd obviously earned them back. So we went out into the garage and brought her toys out."

Mel told me that Norah didn't really seem surprised by any of it, even after she reminded her of the missing baby dolls. Norah acted like she didn't remember any of it. Or perhaps she didn't even care to remember the day they were taken away. This is one of the major reasons parenting small children is so frustrating. They only seem to remember about half of what you tell them, and what they do remember is often strange and distorted.

I went into the living room, and Norah was cradling a stuffed puppy that she'd wrapped in a blanket.

"What's your baby's name?" I asked.

Norah thought for a moment. She was holding a swaddled puppy in one hand. And as she thought, she mindlessly rubbed her other hand against her blue puffy dress.

"Monster Fart Pants," she said.

"Wow!" I said. "What a beautiful name."

"This is my favorite baby," she said.

"Do you know who gave you that stuffed puppy," I said.

Norah thought about it for a moment. "Nope."

"It was me. I brought it home for you after my trip to Washington DC. I saw it in a store and thought, 'Norah would love that because she loves puppies.' So I brought it for you."

Norah smiled. "I do remember." Then she dropped the stuffed puppy and did one of her signature jumping hugs.

"You're just a cute daddy," she said. "The best daddy."

I thought about Mel taking away Norah's toys and how it didn't faze Norah. I thought about how Mel will most likely always be Norah's favorite. I wanted to ask Norah if I was better than Mommy because I'd gotten her that puppy a year earlier. I wanted to see if I could get her to say that I was the cooler parent. But it isn't really about that. I need to remind myself that it isn't a competition. It's about having a significant relationship. It's about making sure that your kids know that you love them.

So I didn't say anything. I just let her give me a big hug, felt a warmth in my heart that only little kids can provide, and said, "I love you, too. You're a sweet kid."

And once the hug was done, I watched Norah pick the puppy back up and swaddle it, and thought, "Perhaps being second best isn't so bad."

THE VIRUS

It was 8 p.m. on New Year's Eve, and the whole family was knee deep in boogers. Mel was in pajama pants and a hooded sweatshirt, a boogery, crying baby on her hip. Norah was sprawled out on the sofa, whining for a cup of water, her face pale, cheeks rosy. Tristan was asleep in his bed. And I was sitting at the dinner table, attempting to choke down a bowl of grocery store brand chicken noodle, but my sore throat just wouldn't have it.

Children are little virus sponges wandering around licking toys and other filthy objects. They don't always wash their hands, and they don't always wipe their butts, and sometimes they piss their pants. Kids are the most unclean things I've ever lived with.

The worst is my son. Getting him in the bath is like a full time job. He refuses to pee directly in the toilet, and I have caught him eating dirt. So it wasn't surprising when, a few days earlier, he brought a new virus into the house and infected the whole family. He came home from school with a cold, and a few days later the illness had spread. Suddenly, the whole family turned feverish and cranky and the house smelled like cold medicine and rotting cheese.

Three unwashed and unfolded baskets of laundry from before the illness sat in the living room like artifacts representing the time before boogers ran along everyone's faces, and we only spoke in snorts and coughs. After the sickness spread, Mel and I just stopped giving a damn about the house. Toys were everywhere, along with kids' clothing and random wads of tissue. The beds weren't made, and the floor was littered with toys and food crumbs. Anything outside of sleeping sounded like hell.

"I think I'm dying," I said.

Mel rolled her eyes. "You always say that when you are sick."

"I think it's true this time," I said.

I looked over at Norah lying limp on the sofa. Normally a ball of energy, she laid curled up, not wanting to move. Sickness covered her eyes and flushed cheeks.

It's ironic, really. Most of the time I'd just like Norah to be still for a while rather than bouncing off the walls and trying to climb on me every time I sit on the sofa. I longed for the day that I could relax in a chair without worrying about my five-year-old stomping on my crotch. Even though it was nice for her to be so listless, I felt horrible knowing that she was sick. I wanted to do something to make her feel better.

The same could be said about Tristan, who was wrapped up in a quilt and snorting boogers every couple minutes. An hour earlier, when he first went into his room, I offered him some tissues. He greeted the offer with a straight-faced look of disgust, wiped his nose in his forearm, snorted. "I don't like those."

Normally I would fight him on this, but I just didn't have the energy. Rather I stood there for a bit and imagined how crusted with boogers his bed would be once this was all over.

The person I really worried about, however, was baby Aspen. She'd gone from a sweet, lovable little person to a slimy troll-like creature with a trail of green boogers running down her face. For some reason she felt the need to scream every couple minutes, which made me feel like I took an ax blow to my head. And yet, when I looked at her weeping right eye and the way her chubby arms helplessly gripped Mel's shirt, I couldn't help but feel horrible for her.

We'd had plans to ring in the New Year with some friends who also had kids, but we just didn't feel up to it. I'd managed to drag myself out and get a movie from Redbox, and so we sat around the TV and watched it while eating soup. It wasn't the ideal way to ring in the New Year—I'd probably be in bed by 9 p.m.—but one of the supreme rules of parenting is that you don't get your friends' kids sick. So we were destined to stay home.

Honestly, parenting makes New Year's lame. I hadn't been to an exciting New Year's party since the day my first child was born. Last year, I had a Pokémon party with a group of Tristan's friends. It was great to spend time with my son, but I felt like an f-ing nerd. Before kids, sex was my number one priority. After kids, it changed to getting to bed on time.

Once we got the kids to sleep, Mel and I sat in the living room and discussed how to handle getting up in the night. Mel was sitting in a glider, the baby letting out a bubbly growling sound as she slept. I was sitting on the sofa, legs crossed, head back looking at the ceiling.

"This is the first time we've had all three kids sick at the same time," Mel said.

"I know," I said. "We are at the threshold of hell."

We'd been parents long enough to know that all three kids were going to be whiny little shits, waking up every few minutes to cry, moan, or cough, and ask us to fix something that we couldn't. If Mel and I got through the night without divorcing or committing murder, it would be a miracle.

Mel and I went to bed without really drawing out a concrete plan of attack. For example, in the past we have split the night. One of us takes all the kids until around 2 a.m. and the other taking the rest of the night. Or sometimes we split the kids. Mel might take the baby because she has the milk, while I took care of Tristan's and Norah's needs. However, our negotiations went sour when I suggested that she take the baby and I take the other two.

"I just don't think you want me to sleep at all," Mel said. "You know she will be up more than anyone. I'm so tired."

"I'm tired, too," I said. "I'm just a sick as you are. I'm not trying to be malicious. I'm just trying to come up with a plan."

Neither of us had slept well in the past couple nights. It's funny how lack of sleep and illness can make you blame your partner. If anyone should understand your pain, it's your spouse. They should be willing to work a little harder in the night so that you can feel better, right? Well, yeah. That would be awesome. But in this situation, both Mel and I felt that way, and neither of us was going to budge. After a good hour of arguing, we went to bed around 9 without a plan of attack.

This was a mistake.

An hour later, Aspen awoke. Normally she is a good sleeper, much better than our other two kids. However, this was her first time being sick. She's a binky baby. She doesn't sleep well without it, but this becomes problematic when the kid has a stuffy nose. She couldn't breathe while sucking on the binky, but she couldn't sleep without the binky, which meant a recipe for a long night. Babies are the worst roommates ever.

Aspen kept crying as Mel tried to feed her because she couldn't suck milk and breathe at the same time. This woke up Norah, who cried out, "I have boogers!" She said the last bit of the sentence at a higher pitch than the first in an effort to give the situation sincerity.

I got up and tried to get Norah to blow her nose. But she was too sick and only half awake to figure it out, so she started screaming, which woke up her brother and agitated her baby sister. Tristan did little more than moan in his bed and ask for a popsicle. At the time, I just assumed he was being gluttonous, but in hindsight I have to assume the popsicle was to make his sore throat feel better.

I calmed Norah down and then argued with Tristan for some time about how I wasn't going to give him a popsicle at 11 p.m. He kept repeating the phrase, "But I just want one!" As he cried, I seriously considered climbing in our van, driving to the woods, and sleeping beneath a pine tree.

Most of the time having three kids is wonderful. They are sweet and snuggly and they are always happy to see me when I get home. However, the domino effect of children waking each other in the night when sick is a little slice of hell.

Around 1 a.m. I managed to get Tristan and Norah to sleep. The next few hours consisted of light dozing, a baby crying in the background, and coughing. Mel woke me around 3 a.m. to let me know that the baby had been up the whole time. I couldn't see her face because it was dark, but I could feel her eyes.

"I just want some sleep," I said. "I don't understand why I can't just sleep. Can a person die from lack of sleep? Because I pretty sure that's what they will carve on my tombstone: Clint Edwards, died from lack of sleep (and sex)."

For the next two hours I sat up with Aspen watching *Baby Einstein Lullaby Time* on repeat. The video was about 30 minutes long and consisted of soft classical music by Johannes Brahms, repetitive hypnotic images, and puppets. I'm not sure if it was the cold medicine or the lack of sleep, but around 4 a.m. a plot-less random movie intended to put babies to sleep started making sense. Suddenly I felt like I was on an acid trip.

"Yeah," I said. "I get it. The train moves in a circle."

Aspen fell asleep in my arms around 4:30. I placed her in the crib, and about 10 minutes later she started crying again. I think it was then that Mel and I went from exhaustion to madness. We started to fight about why the baby woke.

"You didn't swaddle her!" Mel said. "She has to be swaddled."

"She wasn't swaddled when you handed her to me, and I couldn't find the stupid swaddle blanket," I said.

We went back and forth, talking about binkies and blankets and everything that probably went wrong that kept the baby from sleeping. Sure, the real problem was that she was just sick and couldn't breathe, but we weren't awake or well enough to be logical. Instead, we just argued.

Eventually Mel took Aspen, swaddled her, fed her a bit more, and placed her in our bed. I climbed in bed with Tristan. And we all slept.

By morning we were tired, but no longer aggravated, and ready to talk rationally. We laughed a little. I can't think of many things more stressful then being up in the night with sick kids. It's a maddening, crazy time. And I am always surprised by how quick Mel and I are to anger in the night and how equally we are willing to forgive each other the next morning.

"I'm sorry for getting so mad in the night," Mel said.

"Me too," I said.

THIS IS WHY WE CAN'T HAVE NICE THINGS

Kids ruin furniture, carpet, and anything you consider valuable. It's a fact. If my kids are not crapping their pants on my sofa, they are coloring on my carpet. To keep them from destroying things, I have made the following crazy decisions.

Pointed a puking child's face at my chest: When Tristan was one, he came down with this horrible puke virus that lasted a week. Until I had a child, I had no idea that a one-year-old could propel puke at a distance twice his own height. I must have cleaned the carpet a dozen times in three days. Eventually I got to where I could see it coming, and once Tristan made the puke face, I pointed his mouth at my chest and let it happen. Now let me just make this clear, I made a conscious decision to allow someone to puke on me because changing my clothing and taking a shower seemed easier than cleaning the carpet or sofa.

Thrown a potty training child with crossed legs onto my lap: Once I was sitting on the sofa and Norah, who was three years old, crossed her legs, place her hands on her crotch, and started to cry. She was potty training at the time. Last time she did this, she wet her pants and got pee all over the carpet. I grabbed her and placed her on my lap. I don't think I need to tell you the rest, but what I will say is, once again, taking a shower and doing laundry was much easier than cleaning the carpet.

Banned Silly Putty: After finding Silly Putty wedged between the cushions of my sofa, it became banned in my house.

Placed a potty training child pinching his butt cheeks into the kitchen sink: During Tristan's first week of wearing "big kid underwear," I found him in the living room with his right hand pinching his butt. He was in shorts, and I wasn't sure if they would hold whatever he was struggling with, so I lifted him up, ran into the kitchen because it was closer than the bathroom, placed him in the sink, and watched him grunt and then smile.

Tackled a three year old with dog poop on his shoes: When Tristan was three, we lived at a small house in Provo, Utah. He and I were playing in the yard when I watched him step in dog poop just outside the kitchen door, and then go running inside. I chased him down, and just before he made it from the kitchen tile to the living room carpet, I tried to reach out and grab him, but ended up falling on top of him. He cried. I got dog poop on my shirt. Then I gagged. If we had recorded it, we would have become a trending GIF.

Spent over an hour cleaning marker off a chair: Once Norah drew all over one of our living room chairs. I got it out, but it took hours of elbow grease and about a million swears.

Wrapped a baby with a blowout in my shirt: In our house, we call a blowout a "code brown." When Norah was a baby, I was holding her while sitting in our easy chair (the only nice piece of furniture we owned). She was in nothing but a diaper. She had a code brown on my lap. I smelled it before I saw it, so I lifted her up and noticed something flowing down her leg.

To keep it from getting on the chair, I hugged her to me. Then I pulled the bottom of my shirt over her and carried her into the bathroom. The teenage version of me would be horrified to know that this is now my life.

Used my bare hands to lift a turd off the floor: One day I was walking through my living room and noticed a turd on the floor. Tristan was potty training, and I had to assume he had an accident. We didn't have a dog or anything. I knew it wasn't me, and I didn't feel right about blaming my wife. I didn't know how long it had sat there, but what I do know is that I was filled with a mix of emotions. Anger that it had happened. Fear that it would stain the carpet. Anxiety about cleaning it up. All of this clouded my judgment and caused me to reach in with no cover, grab the turd, and carry it into the bathroom. Not my proudest moment.

LITTLE BOYS
ARE GROSS

"It was an accident," my seven-year-old son blurted out in the middle of dinner. We all sat at the table eating chicken fingers and fries. Tristan had dried mud on his forehead and knees and hadn't yet changed from his soccer uniform that he wore for his game early that morning. He'd refused to take a bath or take off his shin guards and socks, despite how many times we'd asked him to. I could only imagine what was festering in there after playing soccer for an hour in the rain.

"What was an accident," I asked.

Tristan's face went a little red, and he smiled awkwardly, his dimples showing. "I thought it was a fart."

This was the first time he'd messed his pants in a few years. And I must say, I've run into the "I thought it was a fart," trap many times. I totally understood that the fight was real. Nevertheless, it was gross that he did it at the table.

Mel was sitting next to him. We shared a glance, and then Mel said, "Tristan, why are you farting at the table?"

Tristan shrugged.

"Yeah, Tristan," Norah said. "You are a stinky monster."

All I could think about was the time I crapped my pants in freshmen P.E. Let me just say that when you lose it in gym shorts, you find it in your socks. I immediately looked under the table to see the damage. Obviously it wasn't a full on blowout, but just a little spurt.

"Go to the bathroom," I said. "Make sure it's all out. Then get in the tub."

Tristan looked up at me like I was crazy. Like the last thing that needed to happen was a trip to the bathroom. Like I'd asked him to run a half marathon or, worse, hug me in public.

"I want to finish my fries," he said.

"Hold the phone," I said. "You are planning to sit there in your own crap and finish your dinner?"

Tristan looked confused. He honestly didn't understand why staying at the table after crapping his pants was a problem. This is life with a little boy.

"I don't see what the big deal is," Tristan said. Then he snatched a French fry, and started munching as though the conversation were finished.

"No," Mel said. "I'm not doing this. I'm not sitting next to you with your pants full of crap."

Tristan rolled his eyes. "You do it all the time with Aspen."

"Aspen is a baby," Mel said. "You are a potty trained boy. There is a difference."

Tristan obviously didn't see the difference, which translated to him now feeling picked on. As I watched my son slump in his chair and dig in his heels, I looked at his hands on the table. I thought about how they are my hands. I looked at the stocky shape of his body, his round face, and thought about how much we looked alike. There was no doubt that he was my son, and I wondered if this was how I was at seven years old. Suddenly, I was reminded of a moment with my mother. I don't know how old I was, close to Tristan's age, for sure. I went through a phase where I refused to wipe my butt. It seemed like such a hassle. I hated it almost as much as I hate using the toilet plunger. I didn't get why it was such a big deal. After my father left, my mother worked a lot, which meant I went unsupervised most days. One evening my mother told me that I smelled bad and forced me to take a bath. I fought her on it, so she dragged me into the bathroom, stripped me down, and said, "Oh. My. Gosh. Your butt is disgusting." Then she painfully scrubbed it with a wet rag. This was the first time I can recall feeling embarrassment over my hygiene.

I have to assume that most little boys are just as gross as Tristan. Obviously I was. And I wondered if it would take a moment of shame to get Tristan to clean up his act.

Mel picked Tristan up from his chair, his right hand still holding a fry, and carried him into the bathroom. I heard the water turn on. Mel said things like, "gross," "respect," "decency," "icky," and "ridiculous." Tristan whined, saying it wasn't a big deal. But by the time I heard him hit the tub, he said, "I'm sorry."

I'm not sure if Mel forcing Tristan into the tub rocked his world like it did to me the time my mother did something similar. But what I can say is that Tristan came out of the bath with a somber look of worldliness. He seemed to have experienced something, and as he walked past me, a hooded towel on his head, we shared a glance.

"Someday you'll thank her," I said.

THE ASSHOLE FACE

We call it her asshole face. This is where my five-year-old tilts her head to the side, makes eye contact, and draws her lips to a straight line. Then she does whatever I just told her not to. I tell her not to drink more water before bed, and she gives me the asshole face—and drinks more water. A few days ago Mel was at Tristan's basketball game. Mel told Norah not to go into the other court with her friend, and Norah turned, gave her the asshole face, and kept walking.

Every time she gives me the asshole face, I tell her to cut the crap. "Don't look at me like that," I say. "Who do you think you are?" And sure enough, she does it anyway.

Norah is boy crazy and complicated and enjoys getting her own way. Before becoming a parent I used to listen to my older sister, Melissa, complain about her five-year-old daughter. How she never listened, talked back, and thought she was the boss. I told her that it just showed that her daughter was becoming a strong-willed woman.

"You make her out to be a jerk," I would say. "She's going to grow up and become a CEO or a senator. I think that it's awesome." Melissa gave me a look that seemed to say, *You have no idea what you are talking about.*

And indeed, I didn't. I mean, I love the hell out of Norah. She melts my heart. Her hugs are the sweetest little things ever. But the fact is, she is kind of an asshole right now. I am not going to

89

say that this is a little girl thing because I don't think it is. I think it is a Norah thing. However, I will admit that I often compare her with her older brother and how Tristan acted at her age. What I can say is that Tristan never called me a stupid fart face. He never deliberately ignored me while humming the song "Let It Go." He never tried to manipulate me by fake crying. He never said, "I don't love you anymore" when I sent him into his room or said, "If you make me take a bath, I'll never ever speak to you again." And he definitely didn't have an asshole face.

The sad fact is that my daughter, at age five, is kind of an asshole. I tell her to not talk back and she says, "You can't talk to a princess like that." And the really sad part is, according to her kindergarten teacher, Norah is reserved and soft spoken while at school. While I will admit that I was happy to find this out, part of me wonders if she is only an asshole at home because she secretly hates her parents. I know that some of you reading right now are thinking, "Oh... no! It just means that she's comfortable at home. She feels like she can speak her mind."

Yeah, awesome. Here's the thing: I want her to be confident. I want her to be a strong woman. But there is a difference between being a strong, intelligent woman and someone who crawls around on all fours, claiming to be a puppy because puppies don't have to clean their room. I give her an A for creativity. But at the same time, I want her to understand obligation and respect for authority. Basically what I'm saying is, I want her to do what I ask of her and not make me want to punch myself in the face. I want her to flush her own toilet without throwing a fit, and I want her to clean her room without trying to pull some elaborate animal metamorphosis. I want to somehow channel her thoughts, aggressions, and creativity into a productive form.

I know this all seems overly complicated. I am her father. I should have the power to make her do what I tell her. I am the giver of food, clothing, and shelter. But the sad fact is, my kids have just as much control over me as I do them, and I suspect that Norah fully understands this. I can see it in her eyes. I can see it in the cock of her head. I can see it the way she hugs me and whispers sweet things in my ears.

When I complain about my daughter to other parents they always say, "Just wait until she's a teen." And suddenly I think of when I was a teen and how my teen friends complained about their parents. And how, at the time, something as simple as a curfew seemed unjust. And suddenly I feel like there is no hope. My daughter might just be an asshole until she leaves home.

It's in these dark, frustrating parenting moments that I try to think about the small parenting victories. I think about the times when Norah sits on my lap and I help her with her homework. I think about the smile on her face when she figures out how to read a word, and she immediately seeks out my approval. I think about times when she tries so hard to help with her younger sister or insists on having her mother call me at work so she can tell me about getting a reward at school. I suppose what I'm trying to say is that my five-year-old daughter can be an asshole. Honestly, right now, she is driving me a little crazy. But every once in a while I get a glimpse of her becoming who I know she can be—a bright, responsible person. A strong woman and a passionate, loving daughter and sibling. These moments are what make the complicated mess of parenting, the asshole face for example, worthwhile.

WHAT I SAID I'D NEVER ALLOW MY CHILDREN TO DO, AND THE WAYS I'VE CAVED

Before having children, I had a good list of things I'd never let my children do. I've stuck to some of them, but because of fits or puppy dog eyes, most have gone right out the window. Below are a few examples.

Watch *Barney*: Barney has always scared the hell out of me. He seems like a friendly enough dinosaur, but at the end of the day, once the cameras are off, I know he ate those children. I'm joking (kind of). The point is, substitute whatever show drove you nuts before you had children—*Pokémon*, *Sesame Street*, *Elmo*—and know that my version of that was *Barney*. I always said that my kids would never watch *Barney*. But one visit to the library and they found out about the purple nightmare. We spent hours watching the damn thing. Why? Because when my kids were two or three, Barney got them to shut up for just a moment. It got them to stop clawing at my pant leg or tearing books off my shelf or calling random people on my phone. On those really stressful days, Barney held my toddler's attention just long enough that I could sit down, place my hands on my temples, and keep from going crazy. And for that, I say, bless you, Barney. Eat all the children you want.

Have a messy house: I used to visit homes of families with young children, look at the toys and food on the floor, and think: *What the hell is going on in here? You just don't care?* I didn't know that children are tornados of filth, drool, poop, boogers, sticky goo, and toys. I didn't know about their power to disrupt anything clean. I also didn't know that sometimes it's just better to leave the mess and go to the park, rather than turn into a flaming dictator or spend your days cleaning and missing rewarding moments like trips to the park, wrestling in the yard, or teaching a child how to read.

Play video games: Much like *Barney*, I always said my kids would never play video games. Once my son turned five and discovered that video games were cooler than *Barney*, I found myself in a real pinch. I was in graduate school and sometimes needed to distract him. Suddenly, he started playing games more and more. It is safe to say that his addiction is well regulated. And I will admit that I still don't like games much. But what I can say is that few things get that kid motivated to do anything like taking away his games or granting him more time playing games. This is called true parental power.

Eat at McDonald's: There are so many reasons to hate McDonald's. The food is horrible. Ronald McDonald can't be trusted. The toys and fries are ruining my car. The play area is eerily sticky and smells like pee. I always said I'd never let my kids eat there. But then grandma stepped in. Mel's mother started taking Tristan there. He quickly became addicted to Happy Meals. Before he could speak, he could point at the golden arches and grunt. Then he'd cry when we didn't stop. Now, every time we eat out, both my older kids want to go to McDonald's. They love the place. And frankly, kids have powers, too. When your kids love something so much, even when you think it's gross, sadly you end up there.

Messy backseat: Before kids, I used to look at the backseat of parents' cars and wonder if they were hoarders. Now I understand that kids just don't give a damn about your car. Sometimes it's like the backseat is another country with very liberal dumping laws.

Dress like mismatched hobos: I used to look at kids in mismatched clothing and think: my kids will not dress like that. But then, my kids started dressing themselves. One day, Norah came out in a mixed up outfit that included jeans, shorts, a skirt, clashing colors, flip-flops, and a tiara. She was so proud of her outfit, and I was faced with the choice to support her exploration or squash her independence and make her change. I told her she looked fabulous and took her to the store.

10 CONTRADICTIONS THAT MAKE ME WANT RUN FROM MY MINIVAN AND INTO THE WOODS

My children have a good habit of defying logic. At first I assumed they did this because they hate me. But after eight years and three children, I've learned that children live under a strange code of contradictions that make no sense and are probably the reason many parents drink. Here are a few examples.

1. My children love fries, tater tots, potato chips, and many other forms of potatoes, but if I ask them to eat a baked potato, they will look at me like I placed a hot, steaming turd on their plate.

2. Regardless of how many hours I invested in teaching my children how to wipe their own butts, they still ask me to check if it's clean.

3. My baby refuses to eat most food while sitting in her highchair but will eat anything she finds on the floor.

4. If I put the baby to bed late, she will get up at her usual time or earlier the next day. She does this to spite me.

5. My children ignore me unless I'm on the phone, watching a video online, or going poop. Then they want my full attention.

6. The vacuum, blender, and toilet hurt my son's ears, but he insists on watching *Annoying Orange* at full volume.

7. It takes my children 10 minutes to get all their toys into the living room, and it takes about two hours of bitching to get the toys put away.

8. My baby refuses to poop in the toilet but loves to poop in the tub.

9. Regardless of assigned seating in the minivan, my children fight over who is in "their" seat.

10. If I walk around naked, my kids complain. But if I tell them to get dressed, they look at me like I'm an asshole.

BABIES

I THOUGHT MY WIFE WAS CRAZY. TURNS OUT SHE WAS PREGNANT

When Mel was pregnant with Tristan, we went to the bank to deposit a check. It wasn't a far drive. Just a few blocks. But once we got there, we realized they were closed in observation of some obscure bank holiday that we hadn't considered. Mel was about three months along, with only a small bump below her navel. She'd started shopping for maternity pants but hadn't gotten any yet. Instead, she wore her normal jeans minus a belt. Up until now, the first three months had been more or less like every other month in our two years of marriage.

But as I saw Mel walk up to the bank door, tug on it, realize it was closed, and then tug on it again and again and again, I started to wonder if there was something strange going on. She leaned against the glass, cupping her hands around her eyes to see inside, making sure that there was no one in the bank. As she walked back to the car I realized she was crying, a reaction that seemed extreme, and I wondered if she'd hurt herself tugging on the door.

She opened the car door, sat next to me, and before I had a chance to ask what was wrong, she said, "They're closed because they're stupid. They don't even care. They don't even care." She kept repeating that phrase, over and over, while pounding her fist into her lap. She was really crying now, full on tears with snotty boogers and deep sloppy inhales and exhales. She wiped the snot from her nose with her sleeve, a barbaric action for Mel, something I'd never seen her do before and made me feel like a couple witnessing a war crime, the killing of innocent woman and children, rather than two people simply parked outside a closed bank.

"What's going on, babe?" I asked. I laughed a little, trying to lighten the mood, until she looked at me, eyes wet and slanted, face red and flushed, as if I were now part of the problem.

"Don't be a jerk. These people are closed. I've got so much to do. I'm so tired. And you're laughing at me. Laughing at my pain."

She looked away from me, her fists at her sides, head leaning against the passenger window. It was late fall, cool outside, so her snorting breath fogged the glass. Her hunched shoulders, tense body, irregular breathing, and boogey face reminded me of the lowbrow horror movies I used to watch. Mel was changing. She was turning into something different. Something irrational. Something I didn't know and didn't understand. I got a little scared and thought that perhaps I could reason with her.

"You know, Mel. They'll be open tomorrow. It's no big deal."

She turned toward me, her face flushed, eyes still wet with tears, and said, "No big deal? That gives me one more thing to do tomorrow. One more thing! I've got too much to do. Don't you know that I'm pregnant? Do you even care about our baby? Or me?"

"Well, yeah!" I said. "I know you're pregnant." I chuckled a little. A prideful chuckle. "I put it there."

I smiled at her. I thought I was being funny.

I was not.

"You're a jerk. Did you know that you're a jerk?" she asked. Then she threw her hands up in the air and yelled, "I'm having a jerk's baby."

I didn't know what to do, so I just faced forward, both hands on the wheel with a white knuckled grip, eyes set forward. I don't know what happens to soldiers when they encounter an experience that brings about post traumatic stress syndrome later in life, but I image it is similar to the terror I felt while trapped in a car with my angry, pregnant wife.

I started the car and drove from the bank. And as we drove, she started to calm down as I tried to understand what the hell had just happened.

Slowly, she returned to normal, as though the transition was only temporary. Like the clouds broke and the sunlight had released the demon. We were almost home when she turned and looked at me, exhaling loudly. "I'm hungry. Turn around. I want Taco Bell."

I assumed what happened at the bank was an isolated incident. But then it happened again when I asked Mel to water the Christmas tree. She said, "Don't you know how tired I am? Do you even care how hard it is for me to bend over?" And again when I bought her a steak and she didn't eat it. I got angry because of the cost, and she got angry because I didn't realize that a pregnant woman's taste in food can suddenly change, and a craving can turn to repulsion in a matter of moments. Before Mel got pregnant, our only real fight was over having a baby. And once she was pregnant, we seemed to be fighting about everything from the temperature in the room to who should push the cart at the store. We went from a strong couple to one that fought over petty things, and I honestly wondered if our marriage would survive Mel's pregnancy.

I will admit that the first pregnancy was the most eye opening. Probably because I didn't know what to expect. By the second, I was a little seasoned. I knew to expect mood swings and neurotic behavior. But I have to say that I have found neither experience enjoyable.

Mel's tolerance along with my unwittingly demanding nature was part of the problem. She compromised, which, more or less, meant that she let me have my way. Early in our marriage we watched the shows I liked—*The Simpsons, Family Guy*, and *Arrested Development*. But we never watched *Gilmore Girls* or *Friends*. I told her I couldn't stomach them when, in fact, I'd just never tried. I just didn't want to, and I knew that I wouldn't have to. We ate where I wanted, listened to the music I picked, and set the room to cold so I could sleep.

I chose the first two places we lived in: an affordable first-floor condo where we could hear everything the upstairs neighbors did, from washing dishes to making love, and a small two-bedroom house that was near where I grew up. Behind the house was a hay field, and we always seemed to be having problems with pests—mice, ant, and sometimes demonic-looking goats owned by a neighbor who couldn't seem to mend a fence. But we stayed there because the rent was cheap. In my mind, I assumed we compromised because I'd shown her the places before I signed the lease. But I never let her look for a place. I never asked her opinion. I just told her that this was it. We'd found it! And she accepted it.

Early in our marriage she was not comfortable telling me her thoughts, and I wasn't interested in asking for them. But once pregnant, she spoke her mind. Being uncomfortable and irritated made her happy to let me know about it. The problem, if problem existed, wasn't her mood. She just didn't let me have my way anymore. I interpreted this as her being bitchy and pregnant and derogatory this and derogatory that. But in fact, I was more like a spoiled husband who was not being spoiled anymore.

I never really wanted kids or pets or anything that was dependent on me. I'd meet other people's kids and they'd drool or poo or cry or some other obnoxious thing, and it drove me nuts. But like Mel often does, she broke me down and we had a child. I will admit I really love them. But strangely, I still don't really like other people's kids. I only like my own. I am telling you this so you will understand that one of the major reasons I was so miserable during Mel's first pregnancy was because I didn't really want a child. In many ways, I felt cornered into it. And it is only in hindsight that I realize I was probably just as irrational as she was. I often looked at crying babies and thought about how horrible it was going to be.

Every time Mel wanted to spend money on anything baby-related, I'd get stingy and ridiculous. "Do we really need a car seat? All those safety studies are just propaganda to sell items to unwitting people. The government has no right to tell me how to care for my child!" Or "Why do we need a stroller? I can just carry the damn thing." Each time I said something asinine and irrational, Mel would look at me much like how I looked at her the day she cried outside the bank. Her eyes seemed to say, "Don't you think you're overreacting?" Only she had the good sense not to say it. She must've wondered what she'd gotten herself into. Why did she marry this man? Why had she wanted to have his baby so badly?

It's only when I think back on these moments that I realize something had taken over my body, also. It was a mix of fear, confusion, anxiety, and uncertainty. I attended classes full-time and worked nearly full-time, and I recall having tightness in my chest most days. I woke in the night sweaty, frustrated, and confused. It always came down to money. I really didn't know how to do it. Every day we needed something new—a crib, baby clothing, maternity clothing, prenatal vitamins, bottles, booties, bassinet, Baby Einstein books and DVDs, tub toys, crib toys, living room toys, Vitamin E lotion to prevent stretch marks, and so on.

I remember unwittingly saying the jerkiest things to Mel because I was nervous about money. "Come on, Mel, your feet aren't that swollen. Don't make this out to be more than it is. You can go into work." Or, "Why do we need maternity pants? Just wear some of my pants. You're pregnant. Doesn't that give you the right to look like an overweight hobo?" I recall thinking that I was being funny with that last comment, but it sent Mel running for the bathroom. She locked the door and wouldn't come out for a good hour. When I think back on this moment, I realize that my wife is a saint for putting up with my lack of compassion for what she was going through. She was the one growing a baby. She was the one with swollen ankles and confused hormones. She was the one who got up seven or eight times in the night to pee, only to crawl back in bed and realize that her sciatic nerve was now giving her lower back pain and she couldn't, for the life of her, get comfortable. I was just worried about the check.

When we went to our first ultrasound, I flipped out because our insurance only covered 75% of the cost, leaving us with a bill for a few hundred dollars. "Do we even need to know what the baby's sex is?" I asked. "Can't it just be a surprise? You know, like Christmas."

Mel rolled her eyes and gripped her jeans. Her face was a little swollen around the chin and her skin was spackled with red blotches that she couldn't hide anymore regardless of how much makeup. She was exhausted and miserable, and I think the only thing that kept her going was moments like we were about to have. The excitement of seeing the baby, hearing its heart, feeling its kicks. And I was ruining it.

She drew her lips to a tight white line, looked me in the face, and said, "You're not taking this away from me. I want to know if we are having a boy or a girl. You should, too."

She stopped speaking for a moment and gave me a curt smile. "Stop worrying about money and just get excited. We're having a baby!"

She used this logic a lot. I was supposed to be just as excited as she was simply because we were having a baby. No other reason. But I *wasn't* excited. I was everything but excited. I often thought about how a lesser man could easily cave under the anxiety I was feeling every day and run off. Perhaps it was these same emotions that made my father run off. And sometimes, I worried that I was not a better man than my father. But I loved Mel. I'd never do that to her.

At the hospital, Mel was placed in long reclining chair, something similar to what they have at the dentist's office. She pulled up her shirt and pulled down the stretchy brown cuff of her maternity pants. Her hard, round stomach stuck out, and the nurse coated it with a smooth green jelly. She rubbed a flat-headed wand that was attached to cable, which attached to a screen, across from the recliner.

A blurry, black-and-white image drifted in and out of focus on the screen. The image started to crystalize. I could make out the lips, the nose, and crown. I could see little feet and knees and hips. I could see sockets for eyes and the roll of a small tummy. I could see a baby. My baby. Our baby. There was something about seeing it in the womb that made it real enough to melt my heart. This is just a fraction of what Mel was experiencing. She felt the baby grow inside her. Felt it kick and tug and wiggle and roll around anxiously awaiting for its birthday.

All I'd felt was an occasional kick. Although I knew there was life in Mel's stomach, I don't think I really understood what that meant until I saw it up on the screen. It seemed like a nuisance until then. Someone else's irritating kid. But once I saw the curve of its nose and realized how much it looked like mine, I felt a flood of compassion.

The nurse froze the screen. The she placed an arrow between the baby's legs and typed "boy."

I got really emotional then. I felt very attached. I thought about Transformers, Teenage Mutant Ninja Turtles, Legos, monkey bars, swing sets, video games, candy bars, skateboards, bicycles, monster trucks, the color blue, and the smell of freshly cut grass. I thought about places we could go do, and all the things I could teach him. I was a flood of excitement. It was sudden and overwhelming, like a pulled switch.

We were having a baby! We were having a boy!

Mel started to cry. I got a little choked up myself.

BABY MAKING SEASON

Mel and I were attempting to have a third child, and about three weeks into the baby making, I started looking at my kids and picking apart their frailties. Tristan couldn't seem to flush the toilet. He left floaters all the time. Is that what I wanted? Another floater maker? Norah threw fits. Is that what I wanted? Another fit thrower. Another child sprawled out on the carpet, legs and arms flailing. Sometimes I looked at Norah, assumed she was possessed, and longed for a cross and holy water.

I looked at the messes. Around this time, I shampooed the sofa because it smelled of piss, sour milk, sweat, and Play-Doh. Between the cushions rested dried Silly Putty. I gagged while pouring the thick black sludge from the shampooer trap. It would've been more sanitary to simply set the sofa on fire.

Also, kids need clothes, diapers, and food. They require a car seat, a crib, a potty seat, a crib light for the night, and a car shade for the day. I didn't know how I was going to afford another child. I worked in education. Plus, Mel went green after we moved to Oregon. She proudly showed me environmentally-safe diapers that cost more than regular diapers. I asked her why we needed those, and she replied, "They are better for the environment, and they don't smell as bad as cloth diapers." She scrunched up her nose and made a stinky face. It was supposed to be cute, but I was not in the mood. "It's just our way of saving the planet," she said.

"I'm not trying to save the planet. I'm trying to save money. I'm trying to save my sanity. I feel like you are overcomplicating an already complicated situation. Last time we had a child it was months of you consoling me. Holding me. Telling me that I will be okay. That we can find a way to support the child. That you still find me attractive despite how whiny I was being. This whole diaper thing is pushing me over the edge," I said.

Mel sat on my lap and said, "I know what will make you feel better." She raised her eyebrows.

I looked her up and down, suspiciously. "You don't want me. You just want my baby."

Mel smiled. "Does it matter?" she said.

It was commonly known around our house that we only had what I felt was a sufficient amount of sex when Mel wanted a baby. In fact, the last time she wanted a child I'd never felt so desired in my whole life. Sometimes I'd try and shoo her off so I could give myself a break, but Mel just wouldn't have it.

During baby making season, the rules changed. Sex just happened whether I wanted it or not, and it felt good to be the one to say that I felt bloated after a big meal or that I had a headache or that I was gassy or that I had work to do or that it was too late. It felt good to know that I could turn it down and that it would come back around soon enough. And I suppose in those moments, where Mel was the sexual pursuer, I started to understand why she was so ready to turn me down. She knows that I will just keep wanting her, desiring her, knocking on her door.

Mel downloaded a few iPad apps to help monitor her cycle: My Day's, Period Tracker, Period Diary, etc. My favorite was the Strawberry Pal. This app used strawberries to signify days when she was on her period and bananas to show when she was the most fertile. One of the calendars, I cannot recall which one, allowed her to log how many times we'd had sex that day. Sex showed up as hearts. One day showed two hearts and a smiley face.

"What does the smiley mean," I asked.

"It means I was in a good mood," she said.

"Was it because we had sex twice that day."

"No." She shook her head and scrunched her face like that was a crazy idea. "I can't recall why I was in a good mood that day, but I doubt it had anything to do with sex."

"Glad you're enjoying all this sex as much as I am," I said.

Mel rolled her eyes.

I did the same.

She seemed to be consulting these calendars constantly. Showing me the banana days with a sly smile that seemed to say, *Buckle up, buddy*, and letting me know how accurate this calendar was at predicting her period.

"It was exact," she said. "It knew the very day I was supposed to start." She spoke like the calendar was an intimate friend, a confidant that she could tell anything about our sex life, that it knew everything about her inner workings, and I recall, looking at the sparse hearts and thinking that even while trying to have a baby, we still had a sad amount of sex. Hearts scattered the calendar, one here and one there. Seeing it all visually made me feel pathetic, particularly when I considered how spent I felt.

It happened much faster than I expected. We didn't have any false alarms or several months of anticipation leading up to let down. We didn't have to visit any doctors to ask the difficult question: why can't we get pregnant? In fact, it only took one month of trying. I had mixed feeling about this. I was proud of myself for being so fertile. Clearly I was a lion, a stallion, or some other kid of animal associated with masculinity and sexual prowess. But I was a little let down because I wanted to continue having more sex. I also like the idea of having a little more time to change my mind.

I got the news in Chicago. I was attending a conference for work. I was two hours ahead of Oregon, where Mel was, so I was asleep when she sent a photo to my phone of a little white stick she'd peed on. It said, *yes* in black letters. There was no caption, but none was needed.

I stayed in bed for a while. My boss, David, was sleeping in the bed across from me. Most of the night he sounded like a whale, with his long gargling intakes of air and sloppy exhales. I was tired from traveling and the conference and the long, noisy night. But once I saw the text, I regained some energy.

When Mel told me she was pregnant with Tristan, I sat down in the shower and cried. I was a mix of fear and anxiety. All of it was terrifying, and I didn't know just how to cope with it. I don't think I've ever told anyone about that. When Mel told me she was pregnant the second time, I felt a similar feeling of fear and anxiety, only this time it was not as strong. Nevertheless, I still got real quiet and locked myself in the bedroom for a while. As I write, I am starting to realize how emotional I am. But this time, I just looked at the phone. I wondered if I could handle the sleepless nights, poopy bums, and messy sofas. I thought about how the kids will now outnumber us. They were in control now. I went to the lobby and called Mel. When she picked up I said, "Here we go again."

She laughed.

"Are you okay?" she asked.

"I think so."

I thought about the ebb and flow of my life. I thought about the joy mixed with frustration that children bring.

I went back to my room. David, awake now, wandered around in a red pair of boxer briefs. He was a tall Latin man with a little gray in his hair and trimmed beard. I must have looked different, because he asked if something was wrong.

"We're having another baby," I said.

"Congrats," he said. "You look terrified."

WHAT IT MEANS TO
BE THE FATHER
OF A DAUGHTER

When the sonographer told us we were having a girl I said, "Are you sure you're using that right?"

Mel was in a hospital bed, slightly inclined, her pregnant stomach pushing out beneath her shirt and covered in clear medical jelly. She hit me in the arm.

I was 24, and this was our second child. My question was supposed to be a joke, but there was some truth in what I said. I have one sister, and she's seven years older than me. She felt more like a second mother than a sister. I hadn't spent much time around little girls, so when I did, they seemed screechy and strange. Our son, Tristan, already made a lot of sense to me, and the thought of having another boy felt comfortable. I remember looking at the blurry black-and-white image of our baby. I assumed I was looking at hips. In between them was an arrow pointing, and below it was written, *girl*.

I asked myself, "What does it mean to be the father of a daughter?" And when I thought about that question, I got really scared.

Norah is five now. What I've learned is that being the father of a daughter means a melted heart. It means reading a poorly written book that summarizes the movie *Frozen* every night for six weeks, and although the writing is terrible and I'm sick of the story, I do it because few things are sweeter than having my daughter snuggled next to me. It means driving to work at 6 a.m., alone, and somehow finding myself singing "Let It Go." It means looking at Barbie and wondering if she is setting a bad example of beauty for my daughter. It means looking at Norah's blue-green eyes and realizing that she has as much power over me as I have over her.

When Norah was two years old, she stuck her right hand in a bowl of 400-degree, oven-baked mashed potatoes. She cried loud and hard, and as I sat next to that sweet, chubby-cheeked little girl in the emergency room, listening to her deep wail as the nurse peeled away her soft, dead skin, I cried harder than I did after my father's death. How could I have anticipated that surge of emotion? I'd never wanted to take someone's pain away until then. I'd never felt that before, and honestly, I never want to feel it again. I wanted Norah to be whole. I wanted her to be sweet and wonderful forever. In that emergency room, I never wanted her to feel pain ever again. I felt the strongest need to protect her. And yet, this moment was evidence that I wouldn't always be able to protect her. She would get hurt again someday, and that meant I would hurt, too.

When she had a crush on that young boy at church, I couldn't help but look at him and think, "Norah. You can do better." The moment that thought crossed my mind, I was struck with the age-old question that seems to hit most fathers: who is good enough for my daughter? I got the answer almost immediately, "no one." Yet, I knew that she would one day meet someone and fall in love, and somehow I was going to have deal with that, and I didn't know how.

Having a daughter meant a mix of new emotions that, for me as a man, were completely unexpected. It meant realizing that I, indeed, had a soft side. It meant I wasn't all that tough. It meant realizing nothing was as gratifying as the words, "I *wove* you daddy," and no words stung worse than, "I'm never ever going to talk to you ever again!"

With our third child, Mel had another ultrasound. Sure enough, we were having another girl. Tristan asked if we could change it to a boy, while Norah smiled from ear to ear at the thought of having a baby sister.

The next day it was just Norah and me in our car. We drove home from Tristan's soccer practice. "Let It Go" came on the radio, and Norah sang along in her sweet five-year-old voice. My heart melted like it always does when Norah sings. Suddenly I was struck with the realization that we were going to have another sweet little girl, and I would get to feel this way again. I'd never been more excited.

ASPEN'S BIRTH

"I'm going in to labor." These five words, announced by my wife, scared the shit out of me.

She was up with cramps the night before. I found her in the living room at 5 a.m., hunched over a copy of *What To Expect When You're Expecting*, her right hand holding a flashlight.

"I think I'm having contractions," she said.

But she didn't really know. This was our third child, but Mel had never gone into labor. Tristan was an emergency C-section. And after having one C-section, doctors recommended that Mel have all the other kids that way. Norah's birth was scheduled. And Aspen's was to be the same.

She went on, describing the pain and symptoms she was struggling with.

"I'm going to email the doctor," she said.

Even with the long night and obvious discomfort, she appeared elated. This had been a rough pregnancy, and the thought of getting the baby out early put her in a very good mood.

As she typed on her computer she said, "I just want to be done."

"Should I go into work?" I asked.

"Yes. I'll call you once I hear back from the doctor."

Most of the day was spent looking at my phone and waiting. Unlike Mel, I wasn't as excited for the baby to come early. While she looked forward to feeling better, and I wanted that for her, all

I thought about were the long, sleepless nights. The horrible, fall asleep, get up, fall asleep, and get up nights. I thought about the first two nights in the hospital, when I'd sleep on some shitty fold-out vinyl thing. Beds are in every hospital room, but none are for new fathers. Beds aren't given to fathers. Instead, they're asked to sleep in a chair or on some other piece of cheap, shitty furniture.

I finished up a few emails, told my boss that I was leaving, and then rushed out the door. I work about 30 minutes from home, and by the time I got there, Mel had the car packed up and ready to go. My mother-in-law was in the backseat, and Mel had her hands on her hips, clearly wondering what the hell took me so long.

Indeed, I had taken longer than usual to get home. I do things like that during life changes. Sometimes I wonder if it's a defense mechanism, some primal need to avoid responsibility. For example, I took a back road and got a little lost on the way to my wedding. I usually do these things subconsciously. I'm not even aware that I've made a wrong turn.

We picked up the kids from school and started driving. Because of our HMO, Mel was giving birth in Salem, a 45-minute drive from our house. Our insurance was amazingly affordable, less than $100 a month for the whole family, but everything we needed was 45 minutes away.

Joan, my mother-in-law, the kids, and Mel talked about normal things as I drove. Tristan was going on about his new passion, rubber band bracelets, and Norah was singing a song. They acted like it was any other drive. Mel must have not been in that much pain because she was chatting away, although every once in a while she'd shove a fist into the side of her stomach and cry out.

As we hit the freeway, I started imagining Mel spitting the baby out right there in the car. I'd seen this in movies, scenes where anxious fathers pull the car to the side of the road, lay their wives down along the backseat, use the door frame as stirrups, and deliver their child in some gritty truck stop medical procedure.

While this always seemed funny on film, the bumbling father trying to act like a medical professional, the thought of me actually assisting with the birth of my child nauseated me. I never wanted to do it, so I drove faster.

As we got closer to the hospital, Mel said, "We can park in the parking structure and walk, or we can park in the roundabout outside the building. I took a tour of the hospital, and they said I could park in the roundabout without getting towed."

"Let's park in the roundabout," I said.

"I'd rather park in the structure," Mel said. "That way I can walk some. The doctor said it's good to walk while in labor. It makes the baby come faster."

"No. No," I said. "That's a bad idea. What if the baby just falls out on the ground?"

"My vagina is not a trapdoor."

We parked in the roundabout. The kids stayed with Joan in the waiting room, while Mel and I went into an examining room. Mel stripped down and changed into a gown. She laid down on a hospital bed in the dark room. We chatted with the nurse as she hooked Mel up to this and that, and then we sat there and waited.

So much of giving birth has to do with waiting. Sitting and wondering. As a father, all of this means feeling helpless. Sometimes I'm a cheerleader, other times I'm a bench warmer, but for the most part, I am just there, feeling inactive and worthless.

Perhaps this is why they don't give me a bed.

We met with Dr. Habermeyer, who was well-intentioned and jolly. But as he stuck his fingers inside my wife to see if she was dilated, I couldn't help but feel the urge to punch him in the face. Partly out of jealousy, partly because I felt so helpless and unneeded, that part of me felt like getting pissed would make me feel in charge.

They poked and prodded Mel. They left a cotton swab inside her. They checked readouts. I knew that it was all needed, but at the same time, I hated watching all these people touch my wife. Part of me wanted to scream at them to stop.

Finally, after over an hour, the doctor said, "You are definitely having contractions, but they're mild. I don't think you are going into labor just yet, but I'm going to suggest to your doctor that he move your delivery date up."

And that was it. We were sent home. I told Norah (our four-year-old) that the baby wasn't going to come yet, and she got angry. "No!" she said, "Go tell the doctor to cut Aspen out right now!"

We laughed. But as I looked at Mel's tired eyes, I could tell that she agreed with her. And as we walked back to the car, I was a mix of emotions. Part of me was relieved to not be spending the night at the hospital, part of me was coming down from all the excitement, and part of me was feeling compassion for my wife who looked deflated and worn out, and I wished that she was done being pregnant.

After Mel's false alarm, we met with her OBGYN and he moved her C-section up one week.

The day of Mel's surgery, everyone got up early, around 7 a.m., even though the surgery wasn't until noon. We ate, and packed, and talked about the baby. What she would look like. We announced it on Facebook, "We're having a baby today," and received 300 likes.

And then we went to the hospital. Once again, Mel was stripped down and placed in a gown. She was poked and prodded and hooked up to a bunch of sensors. I was asked to change into a thin white jumpsuit that came with a mask and a hat.

The nurse, JoDee, was in her early 40s. She had highlighted brown hair and a large jaw. She was a straight-faced woman who sat at the computer and asked question after question: "When was your last period?" "Does anyone in your family have a history of this or that?"

"Have you had intercourse in the last 24 hours?" she asked.

"No!" Mel said.

"That would've been awesome!" I said.

Mel rolled her eyes, and the nurse gave me a stone-cold look that seemed to say, "You need to take this seriously."

She gave me the same look after she asked Mel if she'd ever had herpes, and I said, "I'm glad someone finally asked that question."

Before she left the room, I held up the jumpsuit, booties, mask, and hat, and asked, "Do I wear this stuff over my clothes?"

"Yes. I'd really appreciate it if you did."

She hated me, and suddenly I felt the need to explain myself.

"Sorry," I said. "When I get nervous, I make bad jokes."

The nurse gave me a curt smile.

I didn't like a lot of these questions. Way too personal, or flat out rude. In any other situation (work, school, the grocery store) they would be inappropriate. But in the hospital, this wasn't the case. The questions made a stressful situation also uncomfortable, and making jokes felt like the only way to make me feel normal again.

Once dressed, I waited outside the delivery room for an eternity. I sat in a chair, dressed in the jumpsuit and hat, with a camera around my neck. I felt like a tourist in a space suit getting ready to take photos of some bright white planet.

I felt out of place. Then they called me in.

Mel's pregnant stomach bulged out beneath the blue surgical material. Her face was behind a blue screen they'd erected across her chest. This was to keep Mel from looking at the procedure, and I planned to hide behind this screen until the surgery was complete.

A dozen people stood around her, doctors and nurses, I didn't have names for all of them, but I had to assume that they all played some role in the birth. Some held this, others monitored that. I had to assume one was a photographer, the other an agent.

I thought about my earlier fear of Mel giving birth in the car and realized that if that had happened, I obviously would've needed more people.

The doctor placed a scalpel against Mel's stomach, so I looked at the floor. When Tristan was born, the doctor said, "Daddy. Come see your son." I looked around the screen only to see my son half out of a large gaping wound in my wife's stomach.

I almost passed out.

I sat next to Mel. On her head was a tinfoil-looking hat, and her arms stretched out on planks, like she were on a cross. I held her hand, and together, we listened to the pings and pops of the machines, the suction of hoses, and the chatter of everyone in the room. Mel looked nervous and hopeful at the same time.

She was obviously happy to be getting the baby out, but at the same time I think she shared my fear that there would be complications. Norah, our second child, was born with underdeveloped lungs. When she was born, she couldn't cry. She just let out the most pitiful little wheeze. She spent almost two weeks in the NICU. It was a terrifying ordeal. Mel and I both lost a lot of weight from stress, and it caused us to delay having another child for almost five years. This is why, when we heard Aspen cry, we both smiled.

"Did you hear that?" Mel asked.

"Yes," I said. "We should probably get used to that sound. We're going to be hearing a lot of it."

Mel smiled.

Aspen was born on May 8th. She was 7lb 5 oz.

She was covered with a surprising amount of white crud, much more than our previous kids, and as I held her for the first time I said, "You look like a booger."

This was the first thing I said to her.

I think that makes me a poor father.

Aspen made a small O with her mouth and cooed.

The doctor stitched Mel up and the nurses removed the blue surgical material. She was naked, stretched out across a table, people all around her. Below her navel was a large incision. Her stomach was smaller now, and my first instinct was to cover her. But I didn't because I didn't feel it was my place to do so. In any other instance, at any other place, I would've covered her. But for some reason, in a hospital, this seemed strangely normal. Several people helped move her from the surgical table to a stretcher, and Mel smiled the whole time. The nurses made jokes, and she laughed. And all I could think about was the fact that a 7 lb. baby was ripped from her, and now she was naked before strangers, and yet, she smiled.

I've never had surgery. I've never been laid out naked before a group of strangers. I don't even like changing in a locker room. I couldn't help but marvel at Mel's strength.

Mel, Aspen, and I moved to a recovery room. The nurse checked Mel, while I held the baby.

I introduced myself to her.

"I'm Dad," I said. "And her, over there, that's your mom. You have a brother, named Tristan. He's seven years older than you. He might end up being more like a father than a brother. And Norah, she's your older sister. You two will be sharing a room. She has lots of dolls. I'm sure you two will love and loathe each other."

I looked up at Mel. She smiled back at me. "You're a cute dad."

I looked back at her and said, "You're the strongest person I know."

AN OPEN LETTER TO MY NEWBORN

Aspen: I know that you are new to this family. You've only been with us one week. But frankly, there are a few things that need to change if you are going to keep living here. Your mother and I have discussed it, and below are a list of seven changes that you are going to need to make in the coming months.

1. Keep milk inside your body.

Have you seen all the white stains on my shirt? Mom's back has puke all over it. This has to stop. If you need to puke, do it in the toilet. I know that you are often relieved after puking, but puking on someone and then smiling about it is rude. You also wouldn't be so hungry all the time if you'd just keep your food down. This is something you really need to work on.

2. Sleep through the night.

A few nights ago you cried until 3 a.m. Then you slept next to me for one hour in my bed and were up again for another two hours. This is unacceptable. As I was getting ready to go to work at 6 a.m., you fell back into a deep slumber. Then, as I slogged through work after being up with you most of the night, you slept in the living room. This is, hands down, the jerkiest thing that anyone has ever done to me. You're lucky you're cute.

3. Use the toilet.

I don't think this should require an explanation. Changing your bum sucks. Get your shit together (and leave it in the toilet).

4. Lift your own head.

Without my help, your head flops around like a dashboard novelty. I have to make it a point to hold your head at all times. Part of the reason you are so moody is because you can't lift your own head. And sometimes you move your eyes in crazy ways so you can see things. This also makes you moody. And it makes you look possessed. I know gaining control of your own head will take some serious exercise, but you need to figure it out. Stop bitching about tummy time, and build your muscles. No pain. No gain.

5. Tell me what's wrong.

Just yesterday I asked you what was wrong, and all you did was yell at me. I changed your bum, and you still cried. Mom tried to feed you, but you didn't even mention that you weren't hungry. Instead you just punched her in the boob. I wrapped you up in a blanket, but you obviously weren't cold. After an hour of trial and error, you let out a massive, bubbly burp and stopped crying. Why didn't you just tell me that was the problem? Stop making everything a mystery! Just speak your mind!

6. Burp on your own.

Your burps are your responsibility. You need to handle that on your own. Screaming until someone slaps you on the back is strange, *OK*? Knock it off.

7. Go more than a couple hours without eating.

If you just ate larger meals, or heaven forbid you made the leap to solid food, you wouldn't be so hungry all the time. It's also getting a little awkward the way you keep crying (even in public) until mom lifts up her shirt so you can "latch on."

Aspen, I want you to know that I love you. I know that you have some good and some, let's call them, work-in-progress qualities. I hope that you don't think I'm being hard on you, but this really is nothing but basic skills. Your relationship with your mother and me will only get better if you work on them.

Love, Dad

THINGS I DIDN'T KNOW ABOUT BREASTFEEDING: A MAN'S PROSPECTIVE

Our first two kids were bottle-fed, but with our third, Mel breastfed. This was a real learning experience for me. My assumption was that breastfeeding wouldn't be that complicated. Women have been doing it for centuries. Turns out I was wrong. Below are a few things I've learned.

Sometimes they leak: I assumed that breasts were tried and true. They've been around since the dawn of humanity. I didn't realize that the valves leaked. That sometimes, when the baby cries or when it's been too long between feedings, Mel's boobs would start to drip. This really sounds like a design flaw.

Boobs are out most of the day, but not for me: My adolescent dream was for a beautiful woman to hang around my house with her boobs out. With breastfeeding, that dream is real, yet it is much more practical than I expected. Those boobs are not out for me; they are out for the baby. Which is their intended purpose. I understand.

Breastfeeding made our baby hate me: For the first three months of Aspen's life, I was worthless to her. In fact, I was beyond worthless. I was hated. I was an irritation. If I even looked at Aspen for too long she would cry. Forget about holding her. Why did Aspen feel this way? I think it's because I didn't have boobs. I couldn't feed her, so what good was I? Straight up baby daddy discrimination.

Nipples are complicated: Chapped nipples, nipple cream, nipple covers, nipple tension, nipple exposing T-shirts, nipple pads, hidden nipples, leaking nipples. There are so many nipple complications and remedies I can't keep track of them all! Part of the reason this is all so astounding is because, from a pragmatic prospective, my nipples are as useless as artificial plants. They give my body symmetry and sometimes they get cold, but for the most part I don't notice them. They just sit there, on my chest, serving no purpose. I had no idea they could be so complicated.

Boobs get bigger when they are full of milk: This really should have been obvious, but I didn't realize that boobs got bigger when they filled with milk. For me, this really was a catch 22. I will admit that Mel's larger breasts looked nice. However, I feared touching them because I didn't want them to squirt me in the face. This created conflicted emotions of both fear and desire.

Breast envy: The first time I was home alone with all three kids, Aspen woke, started crying, and the tried to latch onto my bicep. I felt completely worthless, and for the first time in my life, I longed for my own set of breasts.

Breastfeeding women like to talk about breastfeeding: Mel chats a lot with her friends about breastfeeding strategy. About covers and products. About moments when someone was a jerk because they were breastfeeding. They talk about breastfeeding much like I talk with my cycling friends about baby powder and ass rashes from spending hours on a bike.

Snuggles envy: I really like snuggling with a new baby. And with our first two kids, I got the opportunity for a lot of snuggle time. But with this baby discriminating against me because I don't have breasts, I often looked at Mel, snuggling with Aspen as she feeds her, and got really jealous.

THE 7 STUPIDEST QUESTIONS I'VE HEARD ABOUT MY BABY

Let's face it, having a baby is exhausting. It makes you sleepy and moody and sometimes, it makes you hate life and everyone around you.

To top it all off, people like to ask obviously stupid questions about the baby. They are always well intentioned, and I always answer them graciously. But after a long night of being up with the baby, there is a sinister side of me that wants to off these people. Here are the seven most frequently asked questions and why they are mind-blowingly frustrating.

1. "You look exhausted. Are you going to try and get some sleep tonight?" Eat my shit! You know what, yeah... I do look exhausted. That's because I was up until 3 a.m. trying to resist the urge to tape the binky to my newborn's face. The rest of the night is a blur of light snoozing, poop, and wet wipes. I will not even try to get some sleep tonight. I will not try to get some sleep for the next year because it isn't going to happen. Shut your stupid face with your quiet bedrooms and only your own butt to wipe in the night.

2. "What's that white stuff on your shirt?" Puke. It's always puke. Tomorrow, there will be puke on my clothes again. If the stain is something other than white, it's probably piss or shit. Deal with it.

3. "Does the baby cry much?" Really? It's a baby. Yes. She cries. All the time she cries. She cries when she's hungry. She cries when she isn't hungry. She cries because she doesn't have the strength and coordination to lift her head off the floor. Most of the time, I don't understand why she cries. Sometimes, I cry.

4. "Are you making sure to help your wife?" You know what, it's the craziest thing. Now that she's had the baby, I just don't care about her anymore. Her job is done. Why treat her like something of value? She had a 7-pound baby ripped from a gaping wound in her stomach (C-section), and ever since she's been home from the hospital, I've been having her spend long hours in the kitchen making me sandwiches.

The answer to your question is, yes! I have been very caring to my wife. In fact, I witnessed what the doctors did to her in order to make this little miracle happen. It was brutal. I almost passed out. And once it was all done, I realized that she's the strongest person I know.

5. "Do you think this will be your last kid?" Don't ask me a question like that. Look at my bloodshot eyes. I'm in the throes of hell right now. Your question is like asking me two weeks after getting food poisoning when I plan to eat at Taco Bell again. Ask me that question in a year.

6. "I know it's not exactly the same, but I got this new puppy, and it's been keeping me up all night whimpering. I totally feel you! We're in the same boat, am I right?"

No. Your new dog is not the same as my newborn baby. You can put your dog in another room, shut the door, and call it a night. No one will think less of you. You can leave it in the yard with some food and a water dish, and it will feed itself. Your dog can walk, eat, and lift its own head without assistance. When it comes to physical development, your puppy is a good year ahead of my newborn. It won't always be this way, but for now, congratulations!

7. "Does the baby look more like you or your wife?" Right now, the baby looks like a shriveled up Papa Smurf with black eyes and wrinkly hands. In three months, she will look like a toothless Alfred Hitchcock. I have no idea who she will look like at this point. But what I do know is that she coos a lot, and it's sweet, and when I hold her, even though I'm tired, I can't help but love her.

THE BABY HATES ME

Mel needed to use the restroom, so she handed me Aspen, our one-month-old baby. Aspen had just finished feeding. She was swaddled in a green blanket, and her eyes were closed. As I held her, she looked content and soft, her little mouth in an O shape.

Then she opened her eyes, saw that I was holding her, and started crying. I bounced her. I tried to burp her. I swung her in my arms. Changed her bum. Nothing. She was pissed. It was always like this with Aspen. Whenever I held her, she cried.

This is because I don't have boobs. Well, I do have man boobs, but not working boobs. This clearly disappoints her.

This problem only surfaced with Aspen. Part of the problem was that this was the first time Mel had ever stuck it out with breastfeeding one of our children. Aspen was our third child. Mel tried to breastfeed Tristan but had to go back to work after a short six-week maternity leave. So we ended up using formula. With Norah, Mel breastfed for about two months, but then doctors found a tumor in Mel's jaw, and the medication she had to take ruined her milk. Once again, we were back to the bottle.

I know that many parents have strong feelings about breastfeeding and how it compares to bottle-feeding. But that is not what I'm trying to argue here. However, what I will say is that bottle-feeding helped me to feel closer to our children early on. They cried, and I felt like I could do something for them. I have to assume that giving a baby a bottle doesn't come close to the bond created by breastfeeding. But for me, this is the closet I can get.

During the first few weeks of Aspen's life, I felt useless. Now that we were more than a month in, I started to assume that Aspen flat out hated me. Every time I was left alone with her, she cried the whole time, regardless of what I did.

Mel was still in the bathroom and Aspen was still crying when Tristan said, "Dad. Let me hold her."

Tristan sat down on the living room sofa. He stuck out his elbows and made a cradle with his arms. I set Aspen in Tristan's lap, and she stopped crying immediately. The same thing happened when I handed the baby to strangers at church.

It was total garbage.

Tristan looked up at me with a shit-eating grin, the same smile he gives me when he proves me wrong or thinks that he's gotten away with something, and said, "She likes me more than you."

What the hell? I thought.

"No, way," I said. "How could she like you more than me? You don't even change your own underwear. Plus, you smell like a fart."

Tristan started giggling at my comment. Then he said, "Aspen likes the smell of my farts."

"No one likes the smell of your farts," I said.

Aspen looked so calm and content in Tristan's arms. I suddenly had a false sense of confidence. I knew that if I picked her up, she would stay calm. I also felt the need to prove Tristan wrong.

I took the baby from Tristan, and she cried again. Tristan smiled at me, and I said, "This proves nothing."

I gave her back to Tristan, and she stopped.

By then Mel was back in the room. She bent down and picked up Aspen. The baby cooed.

Frustration set in. I started having crazy thoughts. I wondered how long this would last. How long would Aspen hate me? Was she my Damien Thorn? Was she the evil child that would, at age twelve, cut my brake cable moments before I left for work? Was she inherently evil?

I was her father. She was supposed to love me, right? *Right?*

Later that night, after the kids were in bed, Mel handed me Aspen. She started crying, and I said, "I think she hates me."

She rolled her eyes. "She doesn't hate you. She's just a baby."

"Then how do you explain the way she stops crying whenever I hand her off?"

She skirted the question. This is usually Mel's way of handling one of my irrational fears.

"Would you mind giving her some vitamin D drops? They're on the microwave," Mel asked.

I went into the kitchen, filled the dropper with vitamins and put a few drops in Aspen's open, crying, mouth.

She licked her lips, and then she cooed. I gave her some more, and she did the same. Instantly, my heart melted. She looked so sweet and wonderful. I flashed back to when I'd given Tristan or Norah a bottle and how connected I felt to them. I felt, for the first time, like I was actually doing something for the baby. Our happy moment didn't last long, but it was long enough to make me feel a little better about the kid.

Aspen still cries when I hold her. I don't know how much longer that will last. But for now, we at least have vitamin time. I give them to her whenever I can. And for just a few moments a day, she is calm and quiet, and I get to feel like she loves me.

5 THINGS I NEVER SHOULD HAVE SAID TO MY PREGNANT WIFE

With each pregnancy, I've said some stupid things that make me very embarrassed. I'm going to have a conversation with my former self. My hope is that some of you future fathers out there can learn from my mistakes

1. "I don't understand why this is making you so tired." Really, Clint? Of course, you don't understand. Why would you even ask that question? The woman is creating a person inside her body. What have you created inside your body? Poop. Pee. Stupid assumptions. How could you possibly understand how tired it makes someone to create a human life? If your wife says she's tired from creating your child, just agree with her. It's a big deal.

2. "Every time I look at your pregnant stomach, I freak out a little." Dude, I am sure that you're scared. Your wife being pregnant represents new responsibility. But here's the deal. Your wife is probably just as scared, and to top it off, she has to look forward to changing hormones, a sour stomach, and pushing an 8-pound baby through the vagina you love so dearly. You are not helping. Try being more supportive. Try getting a little more excited. Kids happen. Don't look to your wife for emotional support. She's got enough to worry about without you moping around and bitching about responsibility. You will be fine. Stop dreading the future and enjoy the moment.

3. "Ugh... why are you crying again?" Stop acting put out. You still have the power to regulate your emotions and hormones. Congratulations. You're not getting struck with sudden sorrow and frustration along with hot flashes and cravings for cheap hot sauce. The closest thing you've had to a hot flash was the last time you ate at Buffalo Wild Wings. And it was a good flash, and the tears you shed were joyful. Stop making the assumption that if your wife is crying it's for no good reason and she needs to toughen up, or some other masculine crap. Just give her hug. Ask how you can help. Let her have a moment or two alone. It's not that hard.

4. "You want Taco Bell *now?!*" The last time you had a craving for Taco Bell at 9:30 p.m., you ran your ass out the door and got a double decker taco. Your pregnant wife wants one, and you bitch. Stop it, you lazy bastard. Go get your wife a burrito.

5. "You are so hormonal! It's driving me crazy." Good job stating the obvious, jackass. Yes, pregnancy makes a woman crazy/weepy/ragey. You knew this. A million people told you, and you saw it on a million TV shows. No surprises. But that doesn't invalidate her thoughts and feelings or mean that something isn't important. Sure, you asked her to water the Christmas tree and she had a meltdown. That doesn't mean you need to act like she has a serious problem. The only problem she has is the baby you placed inside her. That's temporary. She is still the woman you love. You are in this together. Don't react with anger. React with compassion.

18 CRAZY THINGS I SAID WHILE UP WITH THE BABY

Being sleep deprived has caused me to say some crazy things to my baby. I hope she will forgive me.

Here are a few examples:

1. Don't touch my face. I've been up with you for over an hour. We're not friends.
2. I'm changing your poopy butt. *I* should be crying.
3. Stop flapping your arms, you crazy-ass bird baby.
4. This is why Daddy wants to drive into the ocean.
5. Ugh… don't forget about this when you're a teenager.
6. Stop biting me! You're an animal!
7. Stop kicking your legs. I swear I'll get duct tape.
8. Do you see anyone else laughing? It's like you're on drugs. I want some drugs…
9. Normal people don't rub boogers on their face. You're the worst roommate ever.
10. Don't suck there. I'm not built for that.
11. You were asleep! You were asleep! You! Were! Asleep!
12. The stupid binky stays in your stupid mouth.
13. Your diaper smells like apricots. What the hell is going on?

14. This is why you don't have any friends.
15. I cuddle with you, and you push me away. I set you down, and you cry. You're as confusing as your mother.
16. Just tell me what you want! Not everything is a secret.
17. Stop being cute. No one is cute right now. Go the f*%k to sleep.
18. Why are you smiling? Now *I'm* smiling. I hate that we are smiling.

THE NEW BABY IS MAKING EVERYONE ACT CRAZY... INCLUDING DAD

Three days after we took our new baby home from the hospital, Norah pooped her pants.

I stood over Norah, holding Aspen in my left arm. She was sitting down on the potty, pants at her ankles, feet a foot and a half from the floor, a small sliver of poo in her underwear.

"Seriously, Norah?" I said. "Why are you pooping your pants? You are too old for this."

Norah looked up at me, her face a little red, and grunted.

She didn't try to explain herself. She didn't say anything. She only grunted. Like an animal. This scene reminded of two years earlier when potty training her, and it seemed like all she did was sit on the toilet and cry.

"Listen, Norah," I said. "You got this potty thing down. What's the deal?"

She grunted again. Then she pointed at the door.

"I don't answer to grunts," I said. "You want me to leave, then ask me to leave. In English."

She grunted again and pointed.

I folded my arms, letting her know that I was standing firm. I wasn't going anywhere.

I was a rock.

She started screaming. A top-of-her-lungs, hair flapping around crazy scream.

"Fine," I said. "You can clean up your own poo."

I left, and as I did, I wondered if she were reverting to some former state, and I wondered if this had something to do with the new baby. I can't remember Tristan acting strange when Norah was born, but honestly, I don't remember a whole lot from Norah's first year of life because it was also my first year of graduate school.

I'd seen a lot of sitcoms about children struggling with having a new sibling. There was a *Simpsons* episode where Bart struggled when Lisa, was born. Bart cut baby Lisa's hair, and he put her in a box and tried to ship her to another country. But I honestly assumed that it wouldn't happen to us. Tristan and Norah had been so excited to invite Aspen into the family that I assumed this whole new baby thing would be a smooth process. Before we had Aspen, I often imagined our life with a new baby. It mostly consisted of Rockwell-type scenes, where the children simply gazed at the new baby while sporting large, rosy, gap-toothed smiles.

But I was wrong. Thus far, it had consisted of fits, grunting, and poopy underwear.

I stepped into Tristan's room to check on him. His door was shut, so I poked my head in. He was sitting on the floor playing with Legos.

"What are you doing, dude?" I asked.

Tristan didn't respond. Instead, he stretched out his foot and tried to shut the door on my head.

I stepped back into the hallway so he wouldn't hurt the baby in my arms, and he shut the door.

He'd just turned seven and was at that age where he still wanted to snuggle with me on the sofa and kiss his hurts better, but he got embarrassed when I hugged him around his friends. Normally, he's the one trying to get me into his room to check out something he's built or drawn. I was so used to him welcoming me into his little world that this gesture really shocked me. He'd never tried to kick me out of his room before. In fact, I couldn't recall him ever being in his room with the door shut. It's not like the kid has much modesty. He's seven. Without parental intervention, I don't think he'd ever wear pants again. He was too young to be messing around with himself, or at least I hoped he was. I didn't start taking extended showers until I was 11 or 12. And he usually doesn't try to hide when he does something wrong. He's more of a "I have something to tell you, Dad" kind of kid.

This was very unusual.

I started to wonder if he was entering that "I hate my parents" phase early.

"Go away," he said.

I tried to open the door again, but his foot was blocking it. I easily could've forced my way in, but I didn't want to hurt him.

"Tristan," I said through the door, "I've got the baby. You almost smashed her head. And why would you shut the door on my face?"

Like Norah, he didn't try to explain himself, he just grunted.

"What are you?" I asked, "A monkey? No. You're not. You are a boy who can speak his mind. So answer me, why did you slam the door?"

He grunted again.

I tried the door once more, and Tristan screamed at the top of his lungs, "GO AWAY!"

It was loud enough that my heart started pounding.

I didn't know what to do, so I left.

Norah was still in the bathroom changing her underwear. I told her to put her dirty underwear in the garage, and she grunted at me again.

Mel walked past me around the same time.

I asked her how she was feeling, and she grunted. Then she went into the bedroom.

"What the hell," I thought. We have a new baby, and suddenly my whole family steps back a few millennia and starts responding in grunts.

"Ugh, to you too," I said. But she had already closed the door.

I went into the living room. My-mother-in-law was staying with us. She was sitting at the kitchen table with her iPad, one hand on the tablet, the other on her forehead. Joan was in her late fifties, and wearing a blue T-shirt and jeans, her hair a curly brown.

"What's up with Mel?" I asked.

"I don't know," she said. "But she just bit my head off."

Honestly, I kind of expected this from Mel. With our last two kids, she went through an angry phase. I describe it as postpartum rage. I think it is a mix of hormones, sleepless nights, and the pain that comes along with having a 7-pound baby ripped from your stomach.

When Tristan was one month old, we were at the grocery store together. She told me to grab some cereal, but I grabbed the wrong sized box and she called me an idiot. With Norah, she must have yelled at me every day for a month.

All of this is very out of character for Mel. She's a blunt woman when she needs to be, but for the most part she is sweet and soft spoken. The kind of woman who is always smiling.

I sat down on the sofa and wondered how long all this craziness would last. How long would it take to get Norah back on track with her potty training? Was Tristan never going to let me back into his little world? And how long would I have to work around Mel's postpartum rage?

I looked down at Aspen. She was swaddled in a blanket, sleeping.

"I hope you're proud of yourself," I said.

Mel and I took Aspen to the doctor for her two-week appointment. Our pediatrician was a short woman with brown hair and a round waist named Dr. Dodge. She was really friendly and smiley and sometimes, when I chat with her, I think about how much she reminds me of a kindergarten teacher.

Aspen was weighed and examined.

She pooped on the examination table. It seems that all of our kids have done that. It's a real trend in our family.

We asked the doctor about this and that, and then Dr. Dodge said, "How are Tristan and Norah adjusting?"

Mel and I looked at each other. Then I said, "Well...Norah is crapping her pants again. Which is unusual and frustrating. And Tristan has been really quiet and spends a lot of time shut in his room."

Doctor Dodge nodded. Then she said, "Adjusting to a new sibling can be really difficult for little ones. Here is what I suggest. You need to make sure that they feel loved, but sometimes it's best to do it when they aren't looking. I always tell parents to sneak up behind the kids and give them a big hug. Surprise them with it. Fill them with love. See what happens."

In theory, it sounded like a good plan. I wanted to ask her what to do about helping Mel feel better, but I felt it was best not to bring it up while she was around.

Later that evening, I snuck up behind Tristan and gave him a huge squeeze.

"I love you big guy!" I said.

Tristan giggled and said, "I love you too, Dad. Want to see the book I got from the book fair?"

He smiled up at me, and I knew we were good. I was surprised that worked. It was so simple. But frankly, Tristan was an easy kid.

Naively, I assumed that Norah would have the same response.

Norah was putting something in the garbage when I snuck up behind her. I gave her a big hug from behind. She screamed like I was attacking her, so I tried harder. I picked her up off the ground.

"I love you!" I said.

Norah squirmed and screamed louder. Then she tried to kick me in the crotch. (Hopefully that life skill sticks around when she's dating). I set her down, and she looked at me like I was crazy. She stomped her little foot and said, "Daddy! Don't ever do that again!"

"It was a sneak hug," I said. "Dr. Dodge told me to do it."

Norah looked confused at the mention of Dr. Dodge. Then she said, "Dr. Dodge is..." she struggled to find the right word. "A fart-face!"

Then she stormed into her room.

I even tried the sneak-up method on Mel. She was in the kitchen, getting a glass of water. I snuck up behind her and gave her a gentle hug. (She was still recovering. I felt it was best not to try to pick her off the ground like I did Norah.) Then I kissed the back of her neck. "I love you."

"What are you trying?" she asked. "I had a baby a few days ago. It's not going to happen."

"I just wanted to say that I love you."

Mel turned around and looked at me with suspicion, like the only time I ever hugged her from behind was when I wanted sex. Thinking back, sadly, this is probably accurate, but at the time I was offended.

"Show me that you love me by changing Aspen's bum."

She handed me the baby, then she walked away.

At this point I cracked. I was sleep deprived, my kids were fussy, and my wife was recovering. Without realizing it, I started to snap at people. Mel in particular. She asked me why I didn't put her breast covers in the laundry, and I said, "You know... I did a lot of things right today!" When she asked me why I didn't put Aspen's play gym away before I went to bed like she asked, I said, "There's a lot going on right now. I can't remember every stupid thing you tell me."

But much like the kids and Mel, I didn't fully realize that I was starting to act like a jerk. People often talk about how joyful an occasion childbirth is, but actually, it's a good year of regular crying, sleepless nights, spit up, no dates, few family outings, little sex, and arguing over whose responsibility it is to do what. Every time someone says congratulations, it makes me want tell them shut their mouth until the baby is at least a year old. Then you can congratulate me for keeping my sanity and not getting divorced. Making the baby was fun. But surviving the pregnancy and the first year of life, now that is an accomplishment.

The next morning we went to church for the first time with the new baby. We sat near the back of the chapel. Tristan was playing with his bracelet loom, Aspen was asleep in the car carrier, Norah was on my lap, and Mel sat next to me.

Norah asked Tristan for some of the cereal he brought as a snack, and when he wouldn't give it to her, she whined right there in the chapel. She opened her mouth to scream when I grabbed her by the arm and said, "Stop it. Right now. You are acting like a little brat. We are in church. This is not how you act in church."

I'd never called one of my children a brat before. I've thought that they were acting like brats, but I'd never said it out loud. I would've never gone that far. But with the stress of the new baby and the sleepless nights, I obviously was saying things I normally would never say.

Norah may not have fully understood what I was saying to her, but she obviously recognized that I was upset. She got really scared, put her hands over her eyes, and started crying. Then she jumped off my lap and snuggled next to her mother.

Mel placed her hand on Norah's head. Then she gripped my forearm and said, "I know we have a new baby, but that doesn't give you the right to be moody all the time."

"Me?" I said. "I'm the moody one? You and the kids have been the difficult ones. I'm the one trying to hold us all together."

Mel went on, reminding me of all the times I'd snapped at her in the past few days. And then brought up times I hadn't even thought I was acting like a jerk. Clearly all of us were struggling with the stress of a new baby.

"I'm sorry," I said.

"Sorry for what?" she asked.

"Sorry for being so moody. I suppose I'm more stressed than I realized. I'm struggling with having a new baby, too."

We talked for a while. We discussed some of the things we'd been doing over the past few days and how both of us were a mess.

Mel looked exhausted, and I had to assume that I did, too.

"We're in this together," I said.

"Yeah, I know," Mel replied.

Later that night, I read Norah a story. She was in pink and purple PJs, her hair wet and neatly combed. I'd already put Tristan to bed, and Mel was caring for the baby. It was just the two of us. This doesn't happen all that often.

We read *Every Cowgirl Needs a Horse*. Once the story was through and Norah was calm and snuggled up next to me, I told her I was sorry. "I got really angry with you today at church. And I called you a bad name. I'm really sorry, Norah. I know that having a new sister can be stressful, and I'm sorry for being mean."

Norah looked up at me. She smiled and said, "It's OK, Daddy. You just need-a be nice to me."

"I'll always love you. But you know I still have to discipline you when you do something wrong so you won't do those things again. It doesn't mean that I'm being mean. In fact, I do the same thing with Tristan, and I will do the same thing with Aspen. It's just part of being a dad. I will say, though, that when I called you a name earlier today, I was being mean. For that I'm sorry."

I'm not sure if she fully understood everything I'd just told her. But what I do know is that she gave me a big hug and called me a "cute daddy" like she often does when things are better.

I knew that we were all going to still struggle with adjusting to having a new baby, even me. I wasn't the only sane person in the madhouse. Obviously, I was simply a resident. However, I also knew that each day it would get easier, just like it did with Tristan and Norah, and eventually, it wouldn't be new anymore. It would just be life.

Thinking about that made me feel a lot better.

PARENTING IS ABOUT
SHARING THE LOAD:
NO PUN INTENDED

The whole family was at the dentist. Mel, Tristan, and Norah sat in dentist chairs having their teeth cleaned. I was walking up and down the office, bouncing our four-month-old, when I felt something warm and wet on my T-shirt.

I could smell what it was.

Mel and I had gone through several different brands of diapers trying to find one that would contain Aspen's poop: Costco brand, Huggies, White Cloud, Pampers…nothing worked. I'm going to sound like my grandfather here, but we can send a man to the moon, but we can't invent something that can, 100% of the time, contain my baby's crap. If Aspen were an X-Men, her power would be poop. To make matters worse, she looked like the kind of baby you'd expect to drop a major duke. Aspen was a chubby little thing, with rolls in her arms and legs, big cheeks, blue eyes, and a bald head. If placed in a lineup of blowout suspects, she'd be identified as the criminal every time, I assure you.

She had a blowout at least once a day. Sometimes twice. Usually Mel was the one to get crapped on. However, at the dentist, I was the lucky one.

Mel was meeting with the dentist when I asked her where the diaper bag was. It was a large office with multiple dentists and hygienists, and I felt horrible for dragging my poopy baby along the hallways for everyone to smell. Although no one made a comment or even gave me a dirty look, I assumed everyone could see stink lines coming from Aspen and myself. I think few things are as embarrassing as having a child crap on you while in public.

The hygienist, Terra, was bubbly but well-intentioned. She said something snarky about a man changing a baby. As a father, I get this more than I'd like to admit. I don't know if this is a result of fathers refusing to change a poopy baby, or if it's just some social taboo that a man doesn't know how to change a baby. Either way, it's total garbage. If you are reading this and you are a father who refuses to change a poopy baby, knock it off. You are making fathers look bad. And if you are a person who thinks a father can't properly change a baby, stop being a jerk.

By now Aspen was crying. Poop was down her leg, on my shirt, and on my hand. Breastfeeding babies poop like cats. It's disgusting.

Once in the men's room, I quickly realized that there was no changing table. Few things piss me off more than that, particularly when I'm soaking in baby crap. In the seven years that I'd been a father, there had been a lot of forward movement when it comes to adding changing tables to men's rooms. I assume there are fathers out there who get really happy when there's no changing table in the men's room. It means they got out of the job. However, it makes me angry. I'm not saying that I love to change a baby's butt. I don't. But I love my wife and don't think it's fair for her to have to change every diaper when we are out.

I placed Aspen on a sliver of counter next to the sink. I didn't feel right about placing her on the floor. I thought about going out to the car, but before I left, the dentist mentioned that he'd be ready for me in a few minutes. I didn't feel like I had time to walk to the parking lot.

The counter wasn't comfortable for Aspen so she squirmed and cried. To make matters worse, someone (I'm trying not to incriminate Mel here) forgot to put the wipes back in the bag. I used toilet paper, which after using wipes for so long felt like I was performing some *MacGyver* improvisation. This was the first time I'd ever used toilet paper rather than wipes on a baby, and it really showed me how ineffective toilet paper is. I think it only cleaned up about 70% of the mess. I paused for a moment, thought about my own butt, and wondered what I'd been missing all these years.

I cleaned Aspen and myself as best I could. It took much longer than I would've liked, and once I made it back into the dentist, Mel's face held a look that said, "What took so long."

I told her about the blowout and the lack of a changing table. I pointed at the large poop spot on my shirt. I expected compassion. Instead, I got, "It's about time that happened to you."

"Thanks," I said. "Now I feel like a loser."

Mel shrugged. "Getting pooped on every day has made me feel like a loser."

She gave me a forced smile and kissed me. Then she took the baby, and I headed in to get my teeth cleaned.

I sat in the dentist chair, feeling picked on, and I thought about how so much of parenting young kids means feeling this way. Much of it is thankless and messy. It means getting crapped on and then making the best of it. It's about sharing the load, no pun intended.

MARRIAGE

WHAT HAPPENED AFTER WE HEARD OUR NEIGHBORS HAVING SEX

Mel and I were watching a movie while snuggling on a small loveseat in our bedroom the first time we heard the people above us having sex.

We'd been married about three months at the time, both in our early 20s, and living in a small two-bedroom condo in Provo, Utah.

It sounded like loud cliché sex from a movie: squeaking bed frame, headboard slamming, woman moaning, man grunting, and so on. I'd never heard anything like it in real life.

Mel and I looked at each other and started laughing. The people upstairs had just moved in. I was in college at the time, and I'd heard them haul in furniture while I was studying one evening. These condos sat just outside a university, so people constantly moved in and out. When we first moved in I tried to get to know my neighbors, but they kept changing soon after we'd become friends. So by the time the new people above me moved in, I didn't make the effort to run upstairs and meet them because I assumed they'd be leaving in a few months anyways.

As I heard these people having loud, gritty sex, I was grateful I didn't know what they looked like. What if they were unattractive?

"This is remarkable," I said. "Have you met these people? You know, don't answer that question. I don't want to know. If they are really ugly, the image is going to kill me. I will just assume they are supermodels."

Mel leaned to the end of the loveseat and looked up. She was wearing blue jeans with a little dirt on them from her day job at a greenhouse. Her brown hair was shoulder length and pulled back.

"No, I haven't met them," she said. "But this is ridiculous. Our sex doesn't sound like that, does it?"

I thought about it for a moment. I listened to the sounds a little more, and then I said, "Nope. Our sex sounds more like the gentle cycle. Their sex sounds like boots in a dryer."

Mel looked relieved, but this event highlighted how Mel and I had very different sexual expectations. We'd waited until marriage to have sex, and thinking back on those early months, our sex reminded me of two clumsy dancers trying to figure out each other's moves. But to me, the people upstairs sounded like they had real talent.

They'd practiced.

Mel listened with a frown on her face. Her reaction was similar to the face she gave the first time I forgot to lock the bathroom door and she walked in on me. It was one of disgust. She seemed to be thinking: Thank goodness our sex doesn't sound like that. While I, on the other hand, was weighted with this question: Why doesn't our sex sound like that?

I let out my competitive side. "Are we going to let them beat us?" I asked. "We should have a sex war," I suggested. "We should try and out-voice them."

Mel looked at me like I was crazy, like I'd just asked her to have sex on film or something. Like I was out of my mind. Like there was something wrong with me.

"I can't with that going on," she said. "Way too distracting. It sounds like these people are in the room with us. Ugh, this place is so crappy."

She was right. When either of us used the restroom, we could hear it in every room. One evening I was in our living room studying, and I could hear the guy next-door pouring milk on his Rice Krispies.

Snap. Crackle. Pop.

There really were no secrets in that complex. We could hear conversations, screaming children, and now, other people having sex. It made me wonder what elements of our lives others heard. Did the people next door hear us having sex? Did we make them feel better or worse about their sex lives? Did they snicker at us? Did they get frustrated because we sounded like pros?

Sex is intimate, and listening to other people, real people, caused this strange compare and contrast early in my marriage. It made me wonder if we did it wrong.

I looked up and noticed that the ceiling plaster was falling in little flakes due to all the movement upstairs.

Our neighbors had loud sex for about 45 minutes. After about 20 minutes of trying to drown it out by turning on a box fan and turning up the TV, we went into the living room to finish our movie. But we could still hear it. In fact, we could hear it in every room of the condo. Mel finally suggested that we go for a drive, but by the time we got our shoes on, the noises stopped.

"Oh … good," Mel said. "You should go talk to them. Tell them that they need to keep it down."

Was she joking? There was no way I was having that conversation.

"You go talk to them."

I sat on our living room sofa. Mel stood in the kitchen with her hands on her hips. She had a stern look, one that said, *You need to do something*. However, my plan was to do nothing. I never wanted to see those people. I had no desire to know what they looked like. And it sounded like this guy had a good thing going, and in line with man code, I didn't want to ruin it for him.

"Check it out," I said. "These people will be gone in a month, maybe two, max. We've lived here four months, and they are the third neighbors we've had up there. And really, there is no way they can have sex that loud all the time. It's just not natural. He was probably gone in the military, or something, and needed to work off some aggression."

Mel thought about it for a moment. "Sounds to me like he was in prison," she said.

I shrugged.

"Fine," Mel said. "But if they keep it up, you need to do something."

I didn't respond. I had no intentions of doing anything whether they kept it up or not.

Turns out the people above us were sexual juggernauts. They had the same loud sex again later that night, around 10 p.m. And then one more time just after midnight. Mel and I didn't get much sleep. They were at it again, three times the next night, and the night after that. It went on like this for weeks. They never really took a night off, per se, but they did slow down some nights, only doing it once in the evening rather than their usual three time's a charm. Sometimes, however, they did it four times. I assumed this was to make up for the evenings they missed. I assumed they had a quota.

And while the people upstairs enjoyed what seemed like an inhuman amount of angry, loud sex, Mel and I had very little. The whole ordeal had me thinking about sex all the time, but it seemed to be throwing off our groove. I felt bitter. The people had this amazing sex life, while I had jack. But it was early in our marriage, so I didn't know how to broach this subject with Mel. I didn't really know how to bring it up, so I left it alone and hoped, anxiously, for these people to move.

We bought a larger box fan to drown out the noise, which worked for the most part, although it made me wake up with dry sinuses and a sore throat.

Mel kept urging me to go talk to the neighbors, and I kept refusing to. "What am I supposed to say to these people? Something like 'Check it out, we can hear you having really loud sex and, although I hate to ruin a good thing, it's grossing us out. Can you please keep it down?'"

"Yes," Mel said. "That's exactly what you should say. You might even suggest that they put a pillow between the headboard and the wall. Even that would make a huge difference. I'm tired of cleaning plaster off the bedspread."

While Mel is assertive with me, outside of our relationship she is very soft spoken and reserved. She's not the kind of person to confront a neighbor, so I knew that she would never run upstairs and chat with them. Rather, she'd just keep asking me until I caved.

One evening while the neighbors were at it, she did bang on the ceiling with a broom handle, but all it did was make dents. I don't think they could hear it over their headboard.

At the time I was waiting tables at the Olive Garden. For a full month, I'd made it a point not to see the people upstairs. I was terrified that they were really unattractive. Or worse, really old. It was bad enough to hear the people above me having sex, but imagining them as unattractive people was just too much. Instead, I imagined that they were Brad Pitt and Jennifer Aniston, who were still an item at the time. Part of the problem was age. In my early 20s, I made the false assumption that beautiful sex was only something attractive people did. When I think back on this assumption, I realize it is irrational and offensive. Especially now that I am a slightly overweight 30-something with kids. I am the unattractive person having sex, and it isn't gross. It's magical.

I was running late for work one evening. I opened the front door and was about to walk to my truck when I heard the people upstairs open their door. I stepped back inside, shut the door, turned my back to the front window, and waited for them to go down the front steps, get in their car, and leave. However, the two chatted in the parking lot forever.

When my manager asked me why I was 30 minutes late for work, I said that I was trying not to see my neighbors.

"Why don't you want to see your neighbors?"

"Because they have really loud sex, and I don't want to meet them. I'm afraid they might be unattractive."

He snickered, and for a moment I assumed he understood. Instead he said, "That's not a very good reason to be late for work."

This was the first time I'd ever been written up in a job.

Mel and I had discussed moving because of all this, but we had a one-year lease on the condo, while most of the other tenants held a month-to-month lease. We couldn't afford to break the lease, so we felt stuck. I thought about going to our landlord, Greg, but a different person owned each condo in the complex. I really didn't know whom to contact, and I really didn't like the idea of trying to explain this problem to multiple people.

Finally one evening, after listening to the people upstairs for a little over two months and us having very little sex, I decided to approach them. It was just after 10 p.m., and I could hear their TV. Mel and I chatted about it and decided that I would go upstairs and ask them to turn down their show, and perhaps mention that this was not the only thing I could hear.

I knocked on their door. I was nervous as to what I might see. Perhaps the whole apartment would be full of sex toys, blow up dolls, and swings...that sort of thing. Perhaps someone would answer wearing a leather mask with a zipper over the mouth.

I'd started feeling like we lived below an adult film studio.

A man opened the door. He was a little taller than me, probably about 5' 10," with short, blond hair and a small gut. Behind him was a young brunette with curvy hips and a nice smile. The TV was on. They weren't especially good looking, but at the same time, they weren't gross either. In fact, on a scale of one to ten, I would say both scored a seven.

I looked at them for a moment before speaking and realized that my fear of them being really unattractive was completely ridiculous.

I told them that I lived in the condo below, and that I could hear their TV.

"Would you mind turning it down?" I said. "I have to be up in the morning."

This was a lie. I didn't have to be up before 9a.m, but I wanted my concern to sound legitimate.

"Really?" he said.

"Yup," I said. "In fact, I know that you are watching *The Good, The Bad, and The Ugly.*"

"Wow. I didn't think it was that loud."

"I doubt that it is," I said. "The walls are really thin here. I can hear lots of things." I paused for a moment. Then I raised my eyebrows, looked at him and his wife, and said, "LOTS...OF... THINGS."

The man smiled. Then his wife placed her hand over her mouth.

"Oh...I didn't realize," he said.

I nodded, "Yeah..."

We stood in silence for a while. Then I told him thanks and went downstairs.

Mel asked me how it went, and I told her.

"Good!" she said. "I hope they cut it out."

The people above us moved out a week or so later. The sex sounds ended. I can only assume they moved into a cabin in the woods where no one could hear them.

I BLAMED MY WIFE FOR OUR MESSY HOUSE. I WAS WRONG FOR MANY REASONS

I was building shelves in my garage when Helen, a neighbor girl, approached me.

"I just saw in your house," she said. "It's pretty dirty. Norah's mommy needs to clean more."

"Some people find comments like that rude," I said.

Helen looked at me with a snarky smile. "Yup!"

What really sucks about what 5-year-olds say is that they are 100 percent honest. And indeed, our house was a mess. At the time, I could probably have listed a million reasons to explain our clutter piles, random installments of underwear, laundry baskets full of clean laundry sitting precariously in the middle of the living room, and so on. There always seems to be a bracelet loom, a couple dolls, a Play-Doh kit, and a few dirty dishes on the table.

We always have random kids hanging out in our living room or on the porch, eating our food and making messes by getting out our toys and not putting them back. We also just had a new baby, probably the biggest (and best) reason for our messy house.

But none of those excuses really matter because there seems to be no justifiable excuse for having a messy house.

There are people with messier houses. I've seen them. And when I was young, I'd go to these houses and say rotten things like, "I just saw in your house. It's pretty dirty."

Then I'd run home and tell my mother about it, and we'd laugh and judge these messy house people. My mother would say things like, "Doesn't she care about her kids? Or her home?"

It always came down to blaming the mother.

Although we live in an age of partnership and equality, where a stay-at-home dad is not that unusual (in fact, I was one for a short time), no matter what the dynamics of the family, people still blame my wife for our messy home.

I suppose I know this because I, too, used to blame my wife for our messy house.

Shortly after she became a stay-at-home mom, I started getting really judgmental. I started looking at the state of the house and thinking, "You have one job! One job! To take care of the home."

I never considered the fact that kids just don't care if you dust. They'll drop Cheerios anyway. When I was a stay-at-home dad, I'd sweep beneath the table, and 10 minutes later it was dirty again. I'd have the kids put their toys away before bed and by morning, before I even got up, they were back out.

I don't want to speak for your kids, but my kids are remarkable mess makers.

What I discovered was that taking care of the home is actually a collection of many full-time jobs. My wife is a housekeeper, disciplinarian, teacher, nurse, chauffeur, comforter, cook, part-time student, school volunteer, neighborhood caregiver, and more.

A few years ago, Mel and I got into an argument about the house. I told her it was embarrassing. I asked her what she did all day. "It really can't be that hard to keep the house clean," I said.

We got into a huge fight. Mel told me that I needed to realize what she was up against. And then she told me something that really hit home. She said, "Sometimes it comes down to cleaning the house or taking Tristan and Norah to the park. Or spending time having fun with them or teaching them to read or write. Sometimes I can either do the dishes or teach our son how to ride a bike or teach our daughter how to walk. I'd rather do those things, frankly. I'd rather not be that mom who ignores our kids and myself because I'm so busy worrying about what the neighbors might think of our messy house."

I stopped looking at the dirty dishes, assuming that they were evidence of Mel sitting around all day. Instead, I got up myself and started washing the dishes. I realized that this was not her mess, but our mess, and I started pitching in more.

I stopped worrying about the house and started paying attention to the development of our children. I started to pay attention to how happy they were, and the kind of relationship they shared with their mother, and I noticed that we have a messy house and really happy, bright kids.

I'm not saying that if you have a clean house, you are doing something wrong. But what I am saying is that I don't judge my wife for teaching my son how to swim rather than vacuuming the living room. I don't judge her for potty training my daughter rather than clearing the table. And I don't think you should look down on stay-at-home moms with a messy house because, chances are, they are using that time wisely.

SHE SENT ME TO THE STORE FOR FEMININE HYGIENE PRODUCTS

Mel sent me to supermarket with a short list.

- Bananas
- Apples
- Cheerios
- Cottage cheese
- Pads

This was not the first time she'd sent me to pick up a feminine hygiene product. Next to "pads," she listed the brand, weight, length, durability, and a few other details about the specific pads that she wanted. As I read through the modifiers, I was surprised that this was such a complicated thing. Before I got married, I never would've considered that a woman has as many options for hygiene as a car does engine oil.

I felt more uncomfortable than a teenager trying to discretely buy condoms. I waited until the end of the list to pick up the pads. I always do this because it limits the amount of time I have to spend walking around the store anxiously gazing at the hygiene product in the cart, wondering if the people around me are looking at it too, and making assumptions.

And frankly, there are a lot of assumptions to be made.

The normal assumption, and most truthful, is that I'm a married man, sweet and wonderful, and willing to pick that sort of thing up for my wife. But that assumption would take rational thought, which I don't often use in these moments.

Instead, I assume that it shows how whipped I am. Like having those things in the cart while I'm alone shows some chip on my manhood. Perhaps people look at the package in the cart and whisper, "What a bitch for buying those for his wife. He needs to man up." Or worse, I wonder if people are wondering if I'm going to use them as part of some sick sexual fetish.

And while I'm sure Mel wished I better understood what it's like to go through the emotional and physical stress of having a period once a month, I really want her to know what I go through each time she casually places something like this on a grocery list, as if it were no different than picking up a gallon of milk.

Now the last thing that I'm saying is that a woman's period is a 100% equal comparison to a man shopping for his wife's pads. It's not. But what I will say is that buying anything to do with a woman's period makes me feel like I'm giving a public speech to a formal audience while stark naked. It's really a nerve-wracking event.

I stood before the feminine products trying to act casual, like I belonged, but all the while I was a bit red in the face, my right hand shaking as it held the list. I prayed I wouldn't be spotted by anyone who could take a photo. I always assume that I'm going to get better at this with time, that I will become confident to the point that buying pads will truly be as casual as picking up milk.

And I will admit that I have gotten better. The first time Mel sent me to the store for a hygiene product, I felt really nervous, so I bought a bunch of crap I didn't need (a book, some candy, and toilet scrubber) so that I wouldn't look like some creep with nothing but hygiene products in his cart. The cashier checked out my eclectic items, and once she reached the hygiene products, I felt like I need to say something to normalize the situation.

"Don't worry," I said with a smirk. "They're not for me."

The cashier, a snarky, gum-chewing blonde in her late teens, gave me a twisted lip smile that seemed to say, "You know, you saying that makes me think that they are."

Now, after ten years of marriage, I can go to the store, pick out the product Mel needs, strut to the register, and not say a thing. Outwardly, I don't think I come off as that nervous. Obviously, I've gotten better at this, but I still don't like it much.

I found what Mel had listed, and as I tossed it into the cart, I wondered what the male equivalent of this purchase would be. What could I send Mel to buy that would be equally as troubling and embarrassing as me buying her pads? Outside of underwear, my man parts don't require any sort of regular appliance that must be purchased at a store. I can't recall ever sending Mel to get me underwear. And I don't play ball sports, so I can't send her to pick me up a jockstrap.

Perhaps the closest that she's ever gotten was the one time she bought us condoms at Wal-Mart. She came home, a little red-faced and flustered, and told me that condom buying was my job now.

"I'm never doing that again," she said. "Really awkward."

And it's not like I'm not sympathetic to her monthly cycle. But as a man (I think this can be said about most men), I don't think much about a woman's period.

Mostly because I find them a little gross and a little confusing. A few years ago, I went to see the *Vagina Monologues* in an attempt to better understand my wife. I know that the point of the play is to bring about awareness to a woman's coming of age. Let outsiders (men, I assume) better understand what it's like to be a woman, and to allow women an opportunity to normalize and connect over their own coming of age.

I laughed at the play. But at the same time, I felt a little queasy and wondered if any of it would ever make sense to me.

I made it to the cashier with my products. I timed it so that as the pads crossed the scanner, I ran my card through the reader. This made it easier to avoid eye contact. And as I left with my bag of groceries, the pads tucked away where no one could see them, I felt relieved, like I'd just survived a very embarrassing situation (crapping my pants, for example) and made it out without anyone noticing.

Once I made it to the car, I sat in the driver's seat with the engine running for a moment. I thought about my wife and how much I love her.

JUST BECAUSE I GET UP IN THE NIGHT DOESN'T MEAN I DESERVE PRAISE

I was chatting with Mel about the long night we'd had getting up with the baby, when I said, "At least I get up with her. A lot of men don't. You should be grateful."

I was tired. And I said it like she was really lucky to have me. Like I was going above and beyond as a father.

It was just after 7 a.m. Mel paused for a moment, leaned back in the chair, Aspen sleeping in her lap. Her eyes were a little red, and her brown hair was in a loose ponytail. She held the baby a little closer, and took in what I had said. I expected her to agree with me. We sometimes talked about the fathers we knew who didn't get up with their babies. They viewed it as the mother's job.

But she didn't.

Instead, Mel crossed her legs, looked me in the eyes, and said, "I wish you would stop saying that."

At the time, Mel was a nearly full-time college student, a mother of three, and a school volunteer (a requirement of our children's charter school). She spent hours sitting at our kitchen table, hunched over a keyboard, a textbook to her right, and at least one child tugging at her pant leg. And despite her commitment to education, and how much we worked together to care for the home, she often commented on the pressure she felt to keep a clean house- not to mention take the children to the doctor, cook meals, shuttle the kids to sports and other extra curricular activities, keep them looking clean and healthy, and monitor their behavior in public. She was a student and a mother, and yet she felt an enormous pressure to be the sole caregiver of our children. And there I was, feeding into those expectations by mentioning my help in the night as if it were some generous extension of my role as a father.

Naturally, I didn't think about any of this at the time. What I said was my way of trying to get her to notice my contribution to our marriage. As a father, I often feel like I'm really breaking the mold because I do housework. If I'm home from work, I'm cleaning; I get up in the night and do numerous other things to help make our marriage a partnership. But for some reason I felt like I should receive special attention for doing things that have been, for so many years, seen as the mother's job.

I was dressed in slacks and a collared shirt. In my right hand was a purple bag with my lunch. I paused for a moment, took a step back, and said, "Why? I mean, it's true. I do a lot of stuff that other fathers don't. I'm a good guy."

Mel was standing now, the baby in her arms. Our older two children were still sleeping, so we were speaking in whispers. "Because it doesn't make me feel like we're in a partnership. It makes me feel like you want me to kiss your butt every time you get up in the night. This is your baby, too."

We went back and forth for a while. She told me how she appreciated all that I do, but she hated the way I acted like I was doing something really great, when in fact I was just doing what a father should.

My knee-jerk reaction was to get pissed off. I wanted to give her a list of other fathers we knew, family and friends, who still subscribed to antiquated notions of gender roles. I went to open my mouth, but stopped for just a moment, thought about my feelings, and realized it was best to leave before I said something I shouldn't.

So I left for work without saying a word.

I drove to work angry.

I was 20 minutes into my 30-minute commute when I thought about the last time I had washed dishes. I'd assumed that I should be getting praise or a reward, and for the first time I asked myself, *Why? I ate there, too.* Then I thought about vacuuming the carpet, or doing the laundry, realized I had the same expectations about those chores, and suddenly I felt like a jerk. The understanding that Mel was responsible for home and child care was so deeply ingrained in my understanding of family and contribution that I'd placed myself on a pedestal for doing something as simple as getting up with our baby in the night.

By the time I parked and walked to my office, I felt really low.

I called Mel from work, and told her I was sorry. "You're right," I said. "This is a partnership, and I shouldn't act like I'm doing some amazing thing because I get up in the night. I'm going to stop."

Mel was quiet for a moment. Then she said, "Thank you."

HOW MY WIFE HELPED ME TO NOT BE WHITE TRASH

I was chatting on the phone with my old friend Dave. We lost touch 10 years ago but recently reconnected. He mentioned that his youngest son was going to college. I remembered his son as a chubby little boy around seven years old who used to show up to my bike races. Dave asked his son if he remembered me.

"Was he the guy with the long bleached hair and tattoos that swore all the time?"

"Yes. That was him."

Then Dave said to me, "We're all really proud of the changes you've made in your life. You've come a long way from the white trash kid I knew ten years ago."

It's not too often that I get this kind of before and after glimpse into my life. But I suppose Dave was right. I have changed a lot in ten years, and I feel confident that those changes are for the better. But I don't think I would've successfully made any of those changes were it not for Mel's gentle nagging.

She trained me, and I suppose many men might feel that me saying this makes me a pansy, and perhaps I am.

Before I met Mel, I worked full time at a hardware store and was trying to get a job as a prison guard. Most of my paychecks went to tattoos, mountain bikes, and adult entertainment. Now I have two graduate degrees and work at a major research university.

So what am I trying to say? Listen to your wife. She might turn you into something you can both be proud of. But if this testimonial isn't enough, here is a list of things that Mel did to help me become a better man.

1. Supported my educational pursuits: When I first started college at age 22, I didn't know how to type, and I'd never read a novel. I handwrote all of my papers during my first semester of college, and then Mel typed them. However, my spelling was so poor and my handwriting so confused, she couldn't read my writing. We spent a lot of late nights with Mel at the computer and me sitting next to her, reading my paper out loud while she typed.

2. Encouraged me to dress better: When Mel and I met, I was still coming out of a shameful JNCO jeans phase. I tended to wear ill-fitting pants with huge legs and frayed bottoms, holes in the crotch, and burrito stains above the knees. I owned only offensive black T-shirts from punk shows, (shirts that said things like, "Kill a cop for rock and roll") and I was known to take off my shirt whenever possible. Mel started by hemming my pants and encouraging me to buy shirts of different colors. Then we moved into clean pants that fit. It was a long, uphill battle, I assure you. But now I mostly wear slacks and shirts with a collar. I do have mixed feeling about this, however. Few things make you feel old like slacks and a collared shirt.

3. Shamed me into not using bad language: I have a strong mouth. I developed it in my youth. My father had a metal shop in our backyard, and I think I picked it up by listening to his workers. When Mel and I met, every other word out of my mouth was the f-word. Over the years, Mel has made it very clear that using that kind of language is not acceptable—at least not around her, and I can say that it has turned the tide…well, outside of when I get frustrated while working on things around the house, and when my students don't do their assignments and I wind up calling a classroom of college freshman a bunch of lazy f@#*&%. I also tend to use what I call "soft swears." These are the little swear words, such as hell, damn, and fart. Obviously, I still have a lot to work on in this area, but I will say that I have shown vast improvement.

4. Insisted that I shut the door when using the restroom: I used to leave it open; now I don't.

5. Helped me to understand that giving people the finger was an inappropriate greeting: Man, did I think it was funny to give my friends the finger! I don't fully understand why I thought this was so funny, but I did. Mel has a way of convincing me to stop doing embarrassing things through a combination of compassion and moments where she just stares at me, her soft eyes never blinking, her face a mix of irritation and understanding that seems to say, I will break you. It's a clever mix that works every time. This technique really helped me to understand that what I was doing was embarrassing.

6. Mocked me for letting my ass hang from my pants: OK, I'm guilty of not properly wearing my pants. It all started in the 90s. Mel began with mocking me: "I can see your butt crack, and it's not sexy." Then she started trying to pull down my pants each time my butt crack made an appearance. And eventually, she started to drop things into my butt crack (cubes of ice, for example). Sadly, it took years of her doing this before I started to wear a belt and pay attention to where my pants sat before I bent over. But I am happy to say that my ass stays in much more than ever before. I have to assume that the world is grateful.

TRUE LOVE IS NOT HEROICS, BUT RATHER POPPING YOUR PARTNER'S ZIT

I developed a large zit between my right butt cheek and upper leg. It started out as an irritation, but it slowly grew into something so painful that I had to really think twice before sitting down. I was in graduate school at the time, and most days I sat on a hard, uncomfortable wooden desk chair. With a white headed and swollen zit below my butt, graduate classes were intolerable.

I tried to pop it several times but couldn't get two fingers on it. The angle was always wrong. For several days I simply hoped it would go away, but instead it just got bigger. Once it got too painful, I asked Mel if she'd have a look at it. I really avoided this for some time, but I honestly didn't know how I was going to last another day with the stupid thing.

It was evening, around 9:30. The kids were in bed.

Mel wore blue pajama bottoms and a black T-shirt with roses on it. She stood in the living room of the small Minnesota townhome we rented, her hair pulled back and her glasses hanging on her nose, while I was sitting on the sofa at a strange angle, one cheek on the cushion, the other off, grunting a little with discomfort.

Mel's hands sat on her hips.

"Are you asking me to pop a zit on your butt?" Mel asked.

I put up my one hand and said, "No, no. I just want you to have a look at it. Make sure it's not infected, or perhaps a bug of some kind living inside my skin. It's really painful. Now, if you happen to look at it and decide that it's something you could, with your skill set, handle yourself, I would be even more in love with you."

I thought I was being sly and charming. I smiled, expecting Mel to smile back, but she didn't. She was no fool. She knew that I was asking her to pop a butt zit, which has to be the worst kind of zit imaginable. However, I didn't really feel right about asking her directly to do it, so I was trying to beat around the bush.

Before I finally came to Mel with the problem, I'd tried to come up with alternatives. I tried a few kitchen utensils and an old coat hanger. I considered going to the doctor, or even having one of the kids do it. But a doctor visit seemed a bit extreme, and costly, and I didn't want to damage the kids for life by asking them to pop my butt zit. I also didn't have much confidence in the ability of their tender little hands. Coming to my wife with this problem really was a last resort. In a lot of ways, it made me feel like a failure. Like I couldn't handle something so simple or just tough it out until the stupid thing healed on its own.

"Yeah…that's what you're asking," Mel said. Her voice was one of love and compassion. It had a tone of reluctant willingness that showed she would do this, not because she wanted to, but because she loved me.

"Drop your pants," she said.

I stood in the living room, pants around my ankles, with my wife of six years hunching down, glasses hiked up, examining a zit on my butt. She mentioned that the lighting was bad, and as she did, I wondered if this was a deal breaker. If I'd gone too far. If she'd see this as a reason to now find me repulsive. To never have sex with me again because all she could think about when she thought about me was my huge butt zit.

"Holy cow," Mel said. "How have you been walking? It's the size of a silver dollar."

"I know," I said. "It's horrible. Wait, do you think it's worth something?"

Mel didn't laugh. Instead she let out a deep breath, reached in with two fingers, and with a little bit of pressure—POP! It was all over.

"Ugh..." she said. "I hope you realize how much I love you."

Though this was said with sarcasm and frustration, I couldn't help but think of the situation and realize that she did, indeed, love me. Marriage tends to bring about extreme situations where true love and devotion can be tested. In real life, these moments are not always glorious. They are not always a moment of heroics or bravery, but rather moments where one partner does something really unfortunate in hopes of saving the other pain.

I let out a sigh of relief. "You are the most amazing person I know. Yes, I love you."

Mel went into the bathroom to wash her hands while I got myself dressed.

"I'm going to need a doughnut... or something," she said. "I need something sweet to help me forget about this."

"I'll run to the store," I said.

SNORING, HIGH CHOLESTEROL, AND GREEN SMOOTHIES

Mel insisted that I visit the doctor, and while there, I was supposed to ask if anything could be done to keep me from sounding like a suffering whale in the night. I'd ignored the problem for year or so, but once I started waking my children, I felt it was time to do something.

My HMO assigned me Dr. Watson. All I knew about him was a glossy photo. He looked older, knowledgeable, nice. That's the problem with an HMO. Or at least mine. If you want to pick a doctor yourself, it takes days to get an appointment. Take who's available, and you get right in.

I had anxieties about visiting the doctor's office. I gained some weight in graduate school, about twenty pounds, and I was afraid the doctor was going to say that the reason I snored was because I needed to lose weight. I'd never had a medical professional tell me to lose weight, and I really didn't know how I would take it. I assumed not well. I used to consider myself fit. I used to race mountain bikes and bench 350 pounds. I used to look at a body mass index chart and not wish to be six feet tall. I used to eat a balanced diet. People used to ask me for fitness advice.

I used to be sexy.

That is not the case anymore.

Dr. Watson looked a lot like Colonel Sanders, right down to the goofy goatee and mustache. He was about my height, 5' 7," with a large, round belly and stumpy little legs and hands. He waddled, mostly because he was a little splayfooted, and the front of his blue button up shirt was sprinkled with dandruff from his goatee. I kept staring at the dandruff. I wanted to brush it off or, at the very least, suggest he brush it off. It didn't seem right for a doctor to have chin dandruff on his shirt. It didn't seem clean. But we didn't know each other that well, so I just stared at it and said nothing.

He didn't smile much, more of a straight-faced doctor, but he was pleasant enough. He asked me why I needed a physical, and I told him I hadn't had one in a while.

"Anything else going on?" he asked.

"Well..." I said. "My wife wants to know if anything can be done about my snoring."

The doctor scoffed like he'd heard this a million times. Like my snoring was beyond the reach of medical experts. Clearly, I had a problem that couldn't be fixed, which to him meant that the problem was not me, but my wife.

"There isn't much that can be done about that," he said. "Except tell your wife to learn how to sleep through it. Or you can sleep in another room. Some couples do that."

"I don't like either of those ideas," I said.

I noticed that Dr. Watson wasn't wearing a wedding ring. I wondered if he snored in the night and that's why he wasn't currently married. Perhaps he refused to sleep in another room and the tension built due to too many sleepless nights until one day she left, and with her she took all the conditioner, and that's why his chin was so dry and flaky and spackling his nice blue shirt with dandruff.

Was this my future?

He asked me some questions about my snoring. He wanted to know if Mel ever noticed me not breathing in the night. He asked if I had any family members with sleep apnea, and I told him that my brother did. In order to offset his symptoms he needed to wear a mask that forced air into his nose while he slept. It sounded uncomfortable and creepy.

"We probably should get you sleep tested."

"I'd rather not," I said. "If I have this sleep apnea thing, I'd really rather not know about it. I have a hard enough time getting to sleep. I don't know if I've ever actually slept through the night. The last thing I need is a Darth Vader mask chafing my face and keeping me up. Plus, I think it might freak out my kids."

I put my hand over my mouth and started breathing like Darth Vader.

"Wouldn't that sound freak you out as a child?"

I thought I was being funny.

The doctor didn't laugh. He looked up, lips slightly puckered, his face one that seemed to say, *You have no idea what you are talking about.*

"Would you rather wear a mask or take ten years off your life?" he went on. He told me the dangers of sleep apnea, how my organs might be shutting down in the night, which is causing them damage, and suddenly I saw my body like a factory with lazy, unmotivated workers who snuck in extra breaks when the boss was away. This sounded more like a managerial problem. A top-down problem. A problem that could be better fixed with a company teambuilding session in some exotic location. In my mind, what my body (my organs) needed was a company retreat. Not a sleep study.

The doctor told me the story of a patient he once had that died at 27 because he refused to wear his mask.

"Now keep in mind that this man was what we call morbidly obese, close to five hundred pounds," he said.

"Hold the phone, dude," I said. "Are you comparing me to an obese man?"

"No," he said. "I'm using him as an example. Although," he paused for a moment, looking me up and down. Then it happened. He said the statement I was dreading. "Losing weight might help your snoring and your overall health."

When a doctor says that your health could benefit from losing some weight, he's just doing his job in helping you promote good health. This, I understand. However, I found it difficult to not get offended. I had a hard time not looking at this dude and saying, *I need to lose weight? Me? If anyone needs to lay off the KFC it's you, Colonel Sanders. We are the same height and you must have 70 pounds on me.*

The doctor looked me in the eyes. Then he said, "We probably should check your cholesterol."

I went silent, tilted my head back, and looked at the ceiling.

It's not that I didn't work out. I hit the gym five hours a week. Last summer I trained and completed a 105-mile bike ride. And yet, I couldn't seem to lose the weight I put on in graduate school. It's just stuck there. Just before the visit, one of my students said she saw me as a nerdy, fatherly, academic type, and that lifting weights might help me look younger. A few moments later, another student came in, and she confirmed the first student's assessment.

Clearly, whatever sex appeal I had had in my twenties was gone.

I wanted to take those frustrations out on this doctor. I wanted to get pissed off at him, tell him that he needed to lose weight, not me. But my weight gain was not his problem, it was mine, and I needed to accept that.

The real problem was not exercise. It was my diet. It was my love for deep fried chicken. It was my passion for Tyson's frozen foods. It was the fact that I drink five or six cans of soda a day. My poor diet, combined with turning 30 and gaining a sedentary office job, had come down to this moment. It had come down to a medical professional looking me in the eyes and saying that I should lose weight.

I didn't yell at this man. I didn't punch him in the face. I just nodded, and he sent me down the hall to have my blood drawn.

Mel and I were in the kitchen eating lunch the Saturday after my doctor visit. I'd already told her about my upcoming sleep study and how there wasn't much that could be done concerning snoring. But I hadn't told her that the doctor said I needed to lose some weight. I didn't want her to know. Ever since I met with the doctor, I'd felt a little different about myself. I felt older, a little more out of shape. I kept looking at myself in the mirror while pinching my mid-section, and wondering if this fat I'd put on in graduate school would ever go away. I kept wondering if it was defining me.

I ate my usual spicy microwave chicken from the frozen section and drank a Coke Zero. Mel ate a salad and drank water. She stared at her computer, checking our joint email account.

"Oh," she said. "Your test results are in."

At first, I didn't know what she was talking about. I soon realized that she was referring to my blood work. I was a little surprised it was completed so quickly, especially considering how long it took for me just to get a doctor's appointment. I was also surprised that they emailed them to us.

"Let me see those," I said.

I reached for the laptop, but Mel pulled it away from me. Then she looked at me like I was hiding something.

"Just a moment," she said.

She kept reading.

I gave her a moment to read through the email. Then I said, "So am I dying?"

"You have high cholesterol!"

179

She nearly shouted it. Her tone was one of shock and surprise. It reminded me of the tone she used when discovering one of the kids' dirty secrets, like when Norah colored on one of our living room chairs, or the time she found a collection of moldy food under Tristan's bed.

She looked at me for a while without speaking, and I tried to read her face. Mel is a vegetarian. She's the kind of person who shops at the farmers market and often drinks smoothies that mix fruit with vegetables. She's been commenting on my meat consumption for years, but she'd never had clear evidence that it was doing me any harm. But now, on her computer screen was that missing piece.

The testimony of a doctor that proved her case against me.

"How high is it?"

She told me it was about 10 above what it should be. It wasn't dangerously high, but it was still high. She started reading all the recommendations from the doctor's office. It suggested that I get more exercise, eat more fruits, vegetables, and fiber, and cut back on my intake of meat and cheese. This was the worst thing I'd ever heard from a doctor's office. I hated fruits and vegetables, meat was my favorite block on the food pyramid, and cheese was like heaven cut into slices.

"It even says here that making these changes will help you lose weight. Isn't that what you've been complaining about since graduate school?"

I cocked my head back. And that same feeling of anger and frustration that I felt the day before in the doctor's office, I felt again, only this time it was directed at my wife.

I didn't want to change. I just wanted the problem to go away. I didn't want to deal with it.

Mel reached across the table, gripped my hand, and said, "I just don't want you to die. Is that okay with you?"

"I suppose," I said.

Mel started asking me questions about my diet.

"How many servings of fruits and vegetables do you eat a day?"

"Do Tristan's Angry Birds fruit snacks count? I eat those all the time."

Mel gave me a straight-faced look and then shook her head. "No," she said. "When was the last time you ate an apple?"

I thought about it for a long time.

"You can't remember, can you?"

"Nope," I said.

"What about grapes or oranges? I don't know if I've ever seen you eat those."

I reminded her about how eating really juicy fruits causes me to gag. I reminded her of the time she watched me bite into an orange slice and I started uncontrollably heaving.

"I still think that is really strange."

"Tell me about it," I said. "I'm the one who has to live with it."

"What about vegetables. Do you like any of those?"

"Sometimes I eat broccoli," I said. "I also enjoy candy corn." She didn't laugh.

Instead she folded her arms and placed her head on the table like I was hopeless. She sat like that for some time.

Suddenly she sat up, spring-like, and said, "I know what you need! A green smoothie."

"What the hell is that?" I asked.

She walked into the kitchen. She grabbed our blender from the dishwasher, set it up, and starting grabbing things from the bottom of the refrigerator—the crisper. She opened the drawers so casually, and I thought about how I almost never opened those things. I'd always thought of them as Mel's territory.

Mel explained to me that a green smoothie was a smoothie with fruit, ice, and spinach.

"It sounds more like a salad," I said. "Does it have any meat in it? Could we at least throw in a few strips of bacon?"

Mel didn't say anything. She just glared at me.

Then she threw in ice, frozen fruit (peaches, raspberries, and few other colors), and a disturbing amount of spinach. She blended it up, shook the blender with vigor, and blended it again. She poured it into a glass and placed it before me.

The smoothie was thick and green. I sniffed it. It smelled like alfalfa.

"I can't drink this," I said.

Mel sat down across from me. She didn't say anything; she just looked me in the eyes. She does this sometimes. Gives me a look of compassion and wisdom. A look that says, *This is for your own good.* A look that says, *If you love me, you will do this.* A look that says, *Stop bitching.*

The problem is, I am head over heels for her. Which means she has a power over me. I am her bitch.

I thought about Mel's compassion for my health. I thought about my own frustrations with losing weight. I looked at my uneaten chicken on the plate. Then I looked at the green smoothie. Then I looked at Mel.

I took a sip. I rolled it around in my mouth for a moment. It was thicker than I expected, a texture closer to ice cream than a smoothie.

"It tastes like grass."

"Hmm..." she said. "I'll add more fruit next time."

Next time? I thought.

Mel walked around the table, kissed me, and said, "Now finish it. I'd like you to see our grandkids."

I drank the whole stupid thing. Then I threw the rest of my chicken away. And the next day, I packed an apple and some raisins in my lunch.

WHEN SEXUAL INNUENDOS LEAD TO HILARIOUS MISUNDERSTANDINGS

Mel and I usually use sexual innuendos around the house as a way to flirt without the kids knowing what we are talking about. Really anything can be turned into an innuendo as long as it is followed with a sly smile and raised eyebrows. We started doing this shortly after we had our first child. But now that Tristan and Norah are interested in our conversations, our innuendos have created some hilarious misunderstandings.

Below are some examples.

Mel: Thanks for vacuuming out the car. You might just have an appointment tonight.
Norah: Can I go to the appointment?

Mel: I melted the butter for the French bread.
Clint: You melt my butter.
Tristan: Ha! Ha! Mom doesn't have butter.

Mel: Would you mind cleaning the waffle iron? We are having breakfast for dinner.

Clint: I'd like to clean your waffle iron.

Tristan: Mom's waffle iron is broken.

Mel: You suck at loading the dishwasher.

Clint: I'm good at loading your dishwasher.

Mel: No you're not.

Clint: Obviously I am. Look at you. You're pregnant.

Norah: (speaking to Tristan): Daddy's good at loading Mommy's dishwasher.

Mel: We haven't had an appointment for a while.

Clint: Yeah...we should make one for tonight.

Tristan: Is Mommy going to the doctor? Is Mommy sick?

Clint (bending over to pull out a large pot to boil a ham): This stupid ham pot is stuck.

Mel: I like your ham.

Clint: Wow! Thanks, babe. I like your ham, too.

Tristan: I don't like anyone's ham!

Mel: I had a dream last night where we ... played in the backseat.

Me: Awesome.

Norah: I like playing in the backseat. I have toys back there.

Clint: You're invited to the party in my pants.

Mel: (rolls eyes)

Norah: I like parties!

Mel: Are you watching this? You're going to burn the bacon.

Clint: You burn my bacon.

Mel: Nice. Well...I have a paper to write tonight, so you don't get any of my bacon.

Norah: Mommy, can I have some of your bacon?

Clint: What are you putting in that? Corn? I hate corn.
Mel: I like your corn.
Tristan: No one likes Dad's corn!

SOMETIMES MARRIAGE IS GROSS

Marriage is a wonderful thing. I love my wife. I think she is fantastic. But at the same time, after living with her for a decade, I started to realize just how gross people really are. Everything on the list below is natural, I know, but still gross.

1. Your husband will one day crack wind that is so rank you will have to step outside.
2. About three months into your marriage, your wife will run out of toilet paper. She will need you to hand her a roll through the door.
3. Early in your marriage, you will live in a small cramped apartment with thin walls. When someone pees (husband or wife) the sound will echo in every room.
4. During December, January, and February, your wife will go long stretches of time without shaving her legs and/or armpits.
5. One day your husband will ask you to pop a large zit on his lower back, or upper thigh where the leg meets the butt.
6. About one month into your marriage, your husband will casually reach down and scratch himself for much longer than what seems necessary. This will most likely happen

in public: at the grocery store, mall, or church. Once this barrier has been broken, he will begin to scratch at will.

7. Your husband will leave skid marks in his underwear.

8. Your wife will leave sweat stains in her undershirts.

9. One day, as you and your husband snuggle in bed, your husband will fart and then throw the blankets over your head, trapping you in what he calls, "The Covered Wagon." He will think his actions were funny. You will not.

WHY A MOTHER DOESN'T WANT TO BE TOUCHED

I'd gotten home from work around 10 p.m. after a 14-hour day. It was the start of the term, and I was setting up some programs at the university. Mel had been home all day with three sick, boogery, feverish kids.

I walked in, and Mel was at the table, eating cookies and milk while looking at a laptop. She was still in jeans and a t-shirt. Usually by this time of the day she is in PJs, but the fact that she hadn't taken the time to unwind and undress told me she'd had a rough day.

After working 14 hours, the one thing I wanted was a kiss and to hold my wife. When I was in my 20s, this usually meant sex. But now, in my 30s, I'm more interested in simple physical contact with my wife. People often describe me as a people person, but honestly, it's not true. Social interaction feels a lot like acting to me. I'm good at making jokes to disarm a person. But honestly, I often find chatting with others exhausting. With Mel, my wife, I don't feel that. I feel a deep comfort in Mel's arms. There is also something about being at work, sitting across from people, chatting, legs crossed, arms folded, handshakes, and formality that makes me long for some form of real physical contact that I really only get from my wife.

I sat next to Mel, put my arms around her, and kissed her cheek. And as much as I wanted her to turn and embrace me, she didn't. She kept her body slightly rigid, hands forward on the keyboard.

I pulled away.

"What's wrong?" I asked.

"I just spent all day with sick boogery kids clawing at me. I don't want to be touched for a while. I just...want some space," she said.

I felt offended. It made me feel like she didn't love me. I was her husband of 10 years. She should want to be held by me...right? I wasn't one of her children, I was her husband.

"I just wanted to hold you," I said. "I'm not asking for sex, or anything. I'm too tired for that. I'm getting old, obviously. It's been just a long day."

At the mention of being held, Mel cringed a little. Once again, I was offended. I usually am when this happens. And it doesn't happen all that often, but always more than I'd like. But it was late, and I didn't want to fight.

"Fine," I said.

This was not the first time Mel had said that she didn't want to be touched because of the kids clawing at her all day. Honestly, I didn't get it. I don't know if I ever fully will. For me, as a man, it's a difficult thing for me to wrap my head around. I always want to touch my wife. She is the most beautiful woman I know. So much of my attraction to her, my love for her, my passion for our relationship is manifested through physical interaction. At this stage in our marriage, it isn't just about sex. When she kisses me, I feel more confident in our relationship. I feel better about who I am as a man. This became particularly apparent in my 30s. I don't feel as attractive as I once did. I have a difficult time keeping off weight. Not that a lot of women looked at me in the first place, but sometimes they did. But as I've gotten older, I don't get that affirmation like I used to.

I'm also starting to watch a lot of my friends get divorced because they fell out of love. I worry about that. Falling out of love sounds sneaky and organic, like a weed that creeps into a flowerbed. Never in my life has physical interaction with my wife felt more needed as a confirmation that she still loves me. That she isn't drifting away from our relationship because of the stress of raising a family.

When I read what I just wrote, it sounds whiny, but it's the reality of who I have become in my 30s. I feel a deep need for my wife to kiss me and hold me.

We were both in bed now. It was almost 11, an hour after I got home. She slid in next to me, and I put my arm around her.

"It's not you," she said. "It's just…I love the kids. I love you. But all three of them were sick, and I couldn't do anything without the baby clawing at my leg whining, so I held her all day. And Norah, she just wanted to be snuggled." She let out a breath. Then she went on, trying to describe how boogery, drooly, pukey children tugging at her body all day makes her want to crawl inside a bubble. "In the evening, after a long day with the kids, I just want a moment, an hour or so, to not be touched. To just spread out, and not worry about someone pawing at me. It's not that I don't love you, it's just that these days with the kids feel like sensory overload."

And as she spoke, I compared it to how tired social interaction wears me down. I understood what she was feeling just enough to realize that we were at an impasse.

"Does that make sense?" she asked.

"Yes," I said. "It does. I don't like it, but I get it." Then I told her about my day, and how, at the end of it, all I want is to be held.

"I'm not sure if any of that makes sense, but that's how I feel."

Mel crawled into the hook of my arm and rested on my shoulder. I put my arm around her, and we just stayed like that for a while, not speaking.

MY WIFE IS A VEGETARIAN!

I grew up next to my grandfather's beef farm. Cows wandering the open field across from our home, bellowing and whipping their tails, was the backdrop of my childhood. Each fall, Grandpa would pull into my mother's driveway in his gray Chevy pickup. In the back would be several large red sacks of beef, each cut wrapped in white butcher paper: T-bone steak, cubed steak, roast beef, ribs, hamburger, and various other cow parts. He looked a lot like Santa Clause as the old man hauled the large red sack up our steps and into our freezer. I looked forward to these moments.

I have a lot of fond memories of grilling meat as a family. Some of the few good memories I have of my estranged father are of him flipping burgers in our backyard or grilling steak and eggs on the stove. If I got up early enough, he'd cut me off a strip of steak and grill me an egg. Then we'd sit across from each other, not speaking, just savoring the beef.

When Mel told me she wanted to be a vegetarian, I almost shit myself. I looked her in the eyes and wondered if this was grounds for divorce. I thought about all our trips to Sizzler for steak and shrimp. I thought about the day I proposed. After she said yes, we went to Applebee's for steak and potatoes. Anniversaries, birthdays, holidays, graduations, successes, and failures—every significant moment in our life together was accompanied by beef, chicken, or

192

pork. To further complicate things, meat was not only emotionally significant, it was also a symbol of my masculinity. Men eat meat. Men eat a lot of meat because it is what makes us strong. It is the source of our power. Meat put hair on my chest. Meat gave me muscles. My freshman health teacher described using the food pyramid. Meat and dairy stood near the top because, I assumed, they were very important to my survival. When I was sixteen, I bought my first barbeque, a large charcoal grill that came with a side table and instructions on how to smoke a turkey. I'd gotten my first car a few weeks earlier, and I recall thinking that the grill was equally significant. Now I could have friends over and we could grill, bond, and grow chest hair. In so many ways, meat was essential to my masculine identity. And now, eight years in, Mel was changing the dynamics of our marriage. It felt like she was trying to take away something very important to me.

We sat at the dinner table when she told me about her decision to give up meat, and I got a little crazy. I asked her a very silly question that I already knew the answer to.

"Have you tried meat?"

Mel looked confused. "Well, yeah."

"No. No," I said. I shook my hands in front of me, palms out. "I mean have you put it in your mouth? Because it's really good. Anyone who has tried meat wouldn't make this decision."

Mel rolled her eyes. Then she reminded me about some of her health issues.

"The doctor told me that if I eat less meat, I would have less back pain," she said. "So I stopped eating so much meat. Now it is starting to make me sick when I eat it."

I have to admit, what she said sounded reasonable. However, I was beyond reason. Frankly, I was frightened.

Then she told me about watching a documentary called *Forks over Knives*. "It was on Netflix," she said. Apparently, it showed that most, if not all, of the degenerative diseases that afflict us can be controlled, or even reversed, by not eating animal-based foods. She started talking about how healthy a low fat, whole-food, plant-based diet was, and I tried to wrap my head around these new terms, none of which sounded appetizing.

Then she told me about other documentaries that showed the brutality of the food industry. She talked about sad and abused animals, chickens that could hardly walk, living in heaping piles of their own shit, sad and abused pigs, cows being fed corn mixed with steroids rather than hay. What she described sounded very different from my grandfather's farm. He treated the animals humanely. He never pumped them full of steroids and antibiotics. Only hay. For the most part, they seemed to live normal cow lives, wandering about, grazing and pooping. Suddenly, we had very different images of how meat was produced and what it meant. Steak made me think of tractor rides with my grandfather, grilling with my friends, and mornings with my father, while it now made Mel think about cows being filled with hormones and then trapped in a pen, something similar to how Wolverine was created in X-men.

I got scared and said, "Let's cook some sausage and make love. You know. Like we used to."

She didn't laugh. I knew she was serious.

We sat in silence. I was emotional. I knew that if Mel became a vegetarian, I would wind up eating far less meat. I assumed that Mel would be cooking far less meaty dinners, and over the years, I'd begun to really enjoy her meat cooking abilities. I took in a deep breath, and I thought about how difficult it would be for Mel to stick to this diet. We had meat with nearly every meal. This would be a huge shift in her life. I really doubted she could stick with it.

Mel broke the silence. "How about you do it with me?"

I laughed, long and hard, with my hand over my stomach. I took a breath, and I laughed some more. "I've put meat in my mouth," I said. "It's delicious. There's no way."

"You might change your mind if you watched *Forks over Knives*," She said. "It's really moving. I want you to watch it with me."

"Are you crazy?" I asked. "Look what it did to you? No, no. I'd rather not."

Then Mel gave me the look. Her eyes got a little soft as she tucked in her lower lip. She only makes this face when I'm being an ass. I thought about her supporting my return to college. I thought about how she let me do a study abroad in London when Tristan was only one year old.

"Fine. Ok. I'm sorry. I was being a jerk. If this is what you want, I will support you."

Which was only half-true. I ate the meals she cooked. And I tried not to complain when she made me a dried out stick of chicken to go with her vegetarian meals. However, what I did do was try to tempt her. Our evening conversations started with "It's too bad you are a vegetarian because…" and then I'd go on to describe amazing meat-filled lunches I'd had with my coworkers. "We went to this Mexican place and the chicken taco was so amazing my head exploded!" Or, "The burger I ate for lunch had three patties. It was three times as delicious as a regular burger." Or, "They opened a Buffalo Wild Wings next to the university. You would have loved the new sauces." I always held a tone of remorse, almost like I was talking about someone who'd died. This was not something intentional; it just came out that way. And, I suppose, it felt that way, too.

Despite my tempting, despite my remorseful tone, she stuck with it. Until I found her weakness—bacon.

I love bacon. My grandmother raised me, and when I was a kid, she'd make me bacon sandwiches. She'd toast some bread, butter it, and then add about seven or eight strips of bacon. While this sounds like an exaggeration, it is not. She didn't have a problem with it, and neither did I. Sometimes when I ate my bacon sandwiches, I'd feel a pain in my chest. At the time, I didn't pay it much attention. But now I wonder if it was my heart slowing down.

Six months after Mel gave up meat, I started to regularly cook bacon the way Mel liked it best—slowly cooked, crispy, and golden brown. I put box fans in to blow the smell toward her bedroom, and I once wrote, "I love you" in strips of bacon on the counter. One evening as I was making bacon and eggs, Mel walked into the kitchen and said, "That smells really good."

I smiled at her and held the plate forward. I felt sinister, evil, capable of doing anything to get my meat back. I looked her in the eyes as she reached for a strip of bacon, and I smiled slyly, a devil's grin, and thought about a line from Genesis, *When you eat from it your eyes will be opened, and you will be like God, knowing good and evil.*

Mel took a strip of bacon and popped it in her mouth. And as she did, I opened my mouth and my eyes. My face seemed to say, *Got ya!* But I didn't say it. Nor did I point at the bacon and remind her that she was a vegetarian. I held my comments, hopeful that she'd take another strip. And she did. Mel chewed slowly, savoring the moment. Then she gave me a crooked sinful smile that leaned to the one side and I got really excited. I assumed that it was over. I thought about her amazing orange chicken recipe, about her chicken fried steak that was so tender and juicy. I thought about coming home from work and smelling hamburgers on the grill, chicken tenders on the stovetop, and roast beef in the crock-pot. I thought about all the wonders of Mel's cooking and how the last six months had been hell without all these wonderful entrees.

Mel turned her back to me, leaving the kitchen, her jaw chomping down on a strip of bacon. She'd never looked so sexy.

She ate bacon a few more times, munching it down, slyly, and the satisfaction on her face gave me hope that we could go back to our normal, meat eating lives. But it never happened. The only meat I ever saw her eat was bacon.

One evening, as she was preparing a quinoa casserole, I said, "Vegetarians don't eat bacon. You know that...right? Don't you think it is time to stop living a lie?"

Mel turned, placed her hand on her hip, and tilted her head to the side. This is a stance that she only gives me when I have said something outrageously incorrect and she is going to savor this opportunity to set me straight. "Maybe I'm not a vegetarian anymore," she said. She paused for a moment and my heart leaped. I said a little prayer in my mind, thanking God for his intervention.

"I've decided to be a flexitarian." She raised her eyebrows as I placed my face in my hands.

"What the hell is a flexitarian?" I asked. "Can you eat sirloin?"

She told me that it is semi-vegetarianism, and it means that she can have a little meat. We went back and forth for a bit, me listing cuts of meat and her telling me that she still won't eat them. Eventually we narrowed down the list.

"I will eat bacon, sometimes."

"Naturally," I said.

"And I will have ham or turkey on Christmas and Thanksgiving."

"That's it?" I asked.

She nodded.

At first I was pissed. In my head, I called her a hypocrite! I thought about how she needed to be black and white on this. She either was or she was not. But then, a crazy thing happened. The more I thought about it, the more reasonable it sounded. She was really living within her restrictions and only bending her standards occasionally. And I hated that I thought that way. I hated that the way she was sticking to her guns was making me respect her more.

Weeks later I went out for Mexican food with my boss. It was a place I'd never been before, so I studied the menu for a while, looking for a beef burrito or a chicken taco, when my eyes landed on the bean burritos. It sounded really good. Really simple. They made me think of Mel. It was in that moment that I realized I'd started to look at things a little differently. I stopped assuming that a meal needed meat to be a meal.

It's been more than a year, and Mel is still a flexitarian. And, indirectly, I have become one, too. I only eat meat once a day. Sometimes I don't eat meat at all. And sometimes Mel still makes me chicken enchiladas or a bacon burger like she used, too. And I suppose, it has made these moments extra special because I know that she is not making them for anyone but me. It feels like a thoughtful gift that was presented just because she loves me, kind of like when I bring her flowers when she's had a long day.

Mel becoming a vegetarian has really showed how my marriage has changed. How we have grown together rather than grown apart.

WHY I SUCK AT CAR MAINTENANCE

Mel and I took our Mazda to Oil Can Henry's in Small Town, Oregon for an oil change. The sandstone colored siding with bright white trim around the doors, the attendant wearing a small black bowtie and a white collared work shirt with blue stripes, the black wool driving caps, all of it, every detail was to establish the wholesome feel of a full-service 1950s gas station.

We pulled up to the main door, heard a ding inside the shop, and were greeted by an attendant. He had a mustache, and I got the impression he grew it to match the uniform. He waved me into the shop with both hands, occasionally pointing to the left or right, helping to guide my green Mazda Protégé over the pit. Beside me was Mel, and in the backseat was Norah, our four-year-old daughter.

Last time I went to Oil Can Henry's, I got really frustrated with the way the attendant bombarded me with requests for upgrades, so I swore I'd never go there again. But time was short. We were between matches at Tristan's soccer championship (Socctoberfest!), and Oil Can Henry's was the only oil change place in this small town. Also, Mel had nagged me to get the oil changed for over a month, and things had finally come to a head on the drive to the championship.

"Why haven't you gotten the oil changed yet?" Mel asked. "What I am supposed to do if the car explodes?"

"The car is not going to explode," I said. "Stop being dramatic. It's a Mazda. Built to last."

"If you don't get the oil changed I'm cutting you off."

Mel smiles a lot. But when she threatened to cut me off, like she often did, she was not smiling. I knew she was serious.

I went silent for a moment. Then I agreed to get the oil changed between matches.

The irritating thing about Oil Can Henry's is that they don't let you get out of your car. The first thing the attendant did was lean his arm against the top of the car door and ask me to roll down the window. I did, and he handed me a newspaper and a list of services and prices. He was friendly. He smiled. His words carried a whistle followed by a slurp. I assumed this was because there were no teeth in the right half of his mouth, and as I gazed at his lopsided smile, I couldn't help but think of Lube-N-Go back home, in Provo, Utah, where my older brother Ryan changed oil after he graduated high school.

Most of the men he worked with were in their late twenties and early thirties, high school dropouts that knew almost nothing about cars or life or social etiquette. On lunch breaks, they smoked pot behind the shop and then tried to trick coworkers into seeing their genitals. They were single, still lived with their parents, and spent most of their time discussing how the high population of Mormons in Utah was keeping them down. I once heard Don, a 30-something with smelly dreadlocks and a beard that mostly grew from his neck, yell "This town sucks! Damn Mormons. I can't even get a beer on Sunday because of their shit laws. If I could get to L.A., things would be different. People would treat me with respect."

They were morons posing as car professionals. And although Ryan changed oil in Utah, thousands of miles away from where I was, and it was years earlier, I couldn't help but assume that things were the same in this small Oregon town. Within a few moments of meeting the attendant, I already didn't trust him.

"Let's go ahead and check your lights," he said.

The attendant gave me a number of directions. Turn on this. Blinker that. Pop the hood. I could hear another man yelling "check" from behind the car. I waited for it. I waited for him to mention the light, the one that was out above the license plate. The one they always mentioned.

"Light's out above your plate," the attendant said. Then he told me it could be a $250 ticket if I didn't replace it.

I exhaled.

"I can do that myself," I said. Even though I had no intentions of doing so. I just wanted him to leave me alone.

"That light has been out for a year," Mel said, her eyes a little slanted with frustration. "Every time we get the oil changed, they mention it. Do you want a $250 ticket? It's just a few dollars for a light. Stop being lazy."

Mel seemed to assume that car maintenance was part of my manly duties, and she couldn't understand why I wasn't on it. Why I wasn't gung-ho about fixing the car. And when I didn't keep up the maintenance, she assumed it was because I was lazy, but in fact, it was because getting the car fixed was an emotional event.

If I stripped the layers of my mistrust of the attendant, I'd find that the real problem I had with him, and car maintenance in general, was that I didn't really trust myself. I wasn't a car guy. I had no idea how to fix anything, mechanical or otherwise, let alone something as complicated and intricate as a car. I once tried to put a fabricated bookshelf together, and Mel had to take the kids to the park because I was cursing so much. The instructions said to expect 20 to 30 minutes for assembly––that shelf took me more than an hour to complete. It also took one of my fingernails.

Cars were mysteries to me, so whenever I took my car to get it fixed, whether it was a clutch repair or an oil change, I felt like I had to really trust the person doing the work. While in Utah, I didn't have this problem. There my mechanic was my former scoutmaster. I really trusted the guy. But ever since we left home, I've never found an affordable mechanic I can trust. I always assumed they were the same caliber of dumbass that worked with my brother all those years ago. I'd tried to explain this to Mel, but I couldn't seem to find the words, so long ago I decided to just let her think that I was lazy by getting on the defensive.

"This is why I hate taking you with me to get the oil changed. It turns into a lecture. Look at this guy. Do you really think he's a viable source on how much a license plate ticket will cost? I mean, really. $250? Sounds more like the fine for hitting a unicorn. You're stressing me out."

"I'm just asking you to look into it. I'm not saying that you need to have them fix it. Stop getting angry."

"Sure. Whatever. I'll look into it."

"Stop being mean, Daddy," Norah said. "Stop talking. I need quiet time."

Mel went silent, and so did I.

The real problem was pride. I felt like less of a man because I didn't know how to change my own oil or spark plugs or air filters. I didn't know how to fix anything, really. Not without getting really pissed off at myself for not understanding how things work. So I was dependent on other men to do it for me. Men like the toothless, mustached, middle-aged attendant. To complicate things, I was cheap. And I was afraid of getting overcharged because of my ignorance. Men are supposed to be good at fixing things, and for some reason, I have always assumed that I should have an inherent ability to be handy. That I should have been born with a hammer and wrench in my hands, but something went wrong and I was born with a pen and paper. Just thinking about my inability to fix anything makes me feel effeminate.

The attendant shoved a dipstick in my face. "See how burned this oil is?"

"No," I said. "Well... it looks black. Oil is black... right? I don't see the problem."

"That looks icky," Norah said from the backseat.

"You're right, young lady. Back there's a smart kid." The attendant smiled at me, then he chuckled with a bit of twang. More of a "Yuk! Yuk! Yuk!" than a "Ha! Ha! Ha!" Then he rubbed his finger across the dipstick, coating it in oil, and then placed his finger beneath my nose. "Smell it," he said.

I didn't want to, but I felt like I should. It seemed like something a man would do. Was he going to ask me to taste it, too? Was there a point when the attendant stuck his finger in my mouth? (Or somewhere else?) I wondered how far this would go. Was he taking advantage of me?

"It smells like burned toast," I said. "What did you have for breakfast?"

He laughed harder this time, hand over his stomach, and as he pulled his finger away from my nose, he almost soaked my nostrils in oil. "No sir! I didn't have toast. Lucky Charms. That's your oil." He pointed to the sticker in the upper left hand corner of my windshield, the one I got the last time I visited Oil Can Henry's (the time when I committed to never going there again).

"You've gone almost 8,000 miles since your last oil change. We recommend 3,000 miles."

I looked at the sticker and did the math in my head. He was right. Then I looked at Mel. Her wide lips tight. It was her angry face. Then she mouthed, "Eight thousand miles."

Norah repeated what her mother said, only at full volume and with commentary, "Eight thousand miles, Daddy! You need a quiet time."

Mel looked back at Norah, then at me, and said, "You do need a quiet time."

I went limp and tilted my head back into the headrest.

At the time, I was really put out. I did understand Mel's reasoning for wanting a dependable vehicle. After all, one of her biggest fears was to be broken down on the side of some rural central Oregon highway with two small kids in the backseat and a trunk full of quickly rotting groceries. But she felt dependent on me to make sure that the car was, indeed, reliable.

Why? I don't know. There really was no concrete reason for Mel to not be able to take the car to get it fixed. But much like me, I think she dreaded it. This was one place in our marriage where our similarities were a detriment. Like me, Mel worried that a mechanic was going to take advantage of her. But unlike me, it was not because she felt ignorant when it came to cars, it was because she feared that the mechanic would push repairs on her because of her small frame, child-like smile, and friendly disposition. Because she was a woman. And I have to say that I think this was a valid fear. When she did take a vehicle to a mechanic, they seemed to suggest far more repairs to her than they ever did with me.

What it boiled down to was this —I waited until I absolutely had to get something fixed. Mel, on the other hand, felt that the only way she could get something fixed was by cutting me off. Car maintenance really put stress on our marriage.

The attendant told me that I should upgrade my service to the high mileage oil and filter. It was only 20 dollars more, and it would increase the life of my motor. He also suggested gas cleaner, a transmission flush, and replacing a belt. Mel kept staring at me as he talked, and I suddenly felt cornered. Like a caged animal. I thought about other men. Strong men. I thought about characters played by Sylvester Stallone: Rambo and Rocky. My dad wasn't around when I was young, so they were my early models for masculinity. I wondered how Rambo would handle this situation.

"Listen, dude," I said while pointing at the lowest priced service still sitting in my lap. "I get it. I get that you need to upsell me and tell me all about what's wrong with my car. I get that you are only doing what Oil Can Henry tells you to do. But I don't need this right now. Do me a favor. Just change my oil for this price and leave me alone. Is that cool? Is that too much to ask?"

As I spoke, I felt strong. I felt empowered. I felt like a man. I thought about my words, how carefully I placed them, and realized that I probably did sound like Rambo. I even recall thinking that this was probably exactly how Rambo would've performed. *Rambo V: The Oil Change.* The attendant looked at me with sad eyes, his lips a little twisted. He nodded, slowly and sullenly, like I'd just enacted one of his biggest fears. Like he'd been waiting for this day to come. For someone to finally get fed up with his pandering. And in the moment, I felt vindicated. I felt like I'd created a change in this man.

Or perhaps it was a very different emotion. Perhaps he thought we'd grown into friends, and after all this oil change business was over, we would go out and get a beer together. But then I gave him a hard slice of reality.

Or maybe, and I think this is more likely, I was the fiftieth person this week to treat him like shit. To get up in his face for doing his job.

"Yup," he said. "We can do that."

The attendant walked to the front of the car. He crouched below the hood. I looked at Mel who was clearly embarrassed.

"Was that really necessary?" she said. "He's just doing his job. Now he's probably going to cut a hose or a belt or something."

"Great! Now I'm afraid he's going to sabotage the car," I said.

"Well, it'd be your fault."

"My fault? No way. I'm not taking credit for this."

I looked in the backseat. Norah was silently shaking her head, just like I often did at her when she was in trouble. Then she banged her hands into the car seat, "You need a time out, Daddy."

"Norah. You don't even know what's going on."

"Time out!" she screamed.

Everyone in the car was silent for a while. We could hear the attendants below laughing, and I started to wonder what they were doing down there. Norah started to fall asleep.

I looked at Mel. She was searching for split ends in her hair. This was something she often did when she didn't want to look at me.

"Do you think I should apologize?" I said.

"It would be nice. You were kind of a jerk. I mean, how did you like it when people talked like that to you when you were waiting tables at the Olive Garden?"

I waited tables during most of undergrad, and I often criticize people we dine with who treat servers shitty.

"It made me want to spit in their food."

She nodded, "Umm hmm."

I wanted to argue. I wanted to tell her about how I felt uncomfortable there, getting my oil changed. I wanted to tell her how I felt insecure about my masculinity because I don't change my own oil. Perhaps, in this moment I should have made a commitment to change, to become more mechanically inclined. But honestly, I didn't know where to start, and I didn't really want to. I didn't see my life changing. I knew that I'd just go on hating getting my car fixed. I knew that I was dependent on people like the attendant. Perhaps I needed to stop fighting the system and make a few friends. Find some people that I could trust.

The attendant put the hood down with a bang and then came to my window to hand me the receipt. He wasn't smiling this time.

"Hey, man," I said. And suddenly I realized I didn't know his name. "What's your name?"

He looked at me with hesitation, like I wanted his name so I could report him to a manager.

"Scott," he said.

"Scott, listen. I'm really sorry for getting tense with you just a moment ago. I shouldn't have done that. I am sure that I'm like the millionth douchebag to come in here and get pissed at you for doing your job. I don't really have a good excuse for getting angry. Please accept my apology."

"Hey," he said smiling with a little chuckle, "Don't you worry about it. I know that asking people all these questions can be really irritating. I don't really like it either. But I'll tell you what, I really do want your car to run well." He looked me right in the eyes when he said it. There was sincerity in his voice that was unmistakably honest. "You just have a good day and come back and see us."

"You know what, you're a really nice guy."

Scott smiled.

I pulled away.

As we drove back to the soccer match, Norah stayed asleep. It was silent. Mel reached out and held my hand.

EVERY TIME YOU DO THAT I FIND YOU LESS ATTRACTIVE

We were driving to Salem to do some shopping. It was dark out when I casually reached up to my nose, rubbed it with my index finger and, with a ninja-like movement, dug out a booger. Mel turned her head to look out the window, and as she did, I wiped it under the seat.

This was a move I'd done a million times. I turned onto the freeway, feeling like I'd gotten away with something.

"Did you just wipe a booger under the seat?" Mel asked. The scratch in her voice, her clinched fists, her slanted eyes, all told me she was pissed.

"No," I said. "I was just…scratching my nose."

"You are totally lying right now!" she shouted.

I wanted to argue with her. I wanted to put up a fight, but obviously I'd been caught green handed

"If you keep lying," Tristan said from the backseat, "your nose is going to grow and then your boogers will be huge!" Both kids started laughing.

"Huge boogies would be awesome!" Norah said.

We'd been reading a collection of Disney bedtime stories the past few nights. Obviously, Pinocchio had stuck with them.

"Not helping, Tristan. I'm your best friend. Never forget that."

"I only love Mommy," he said, and suddenly I was reminded that Mommy would always be superior in his mind. I hate that fact. This is not to say that I don't love my wife. She is amazing. It's just that, for once, I'd like to be the favorite. I'd like to not be thrown under the bus.

"Great! Now you are being a bad example," Mel said. "I don't care what you do in your pickup, but don't be wiping your stupid booger in my car. I drive this thing every day, and now I have to climb in and worry that a booger is going to be on me. Your booger. Ugh ... it's so gross. Is it really so hard to use a tissue? Do you even care about me?"

I thought about this question for some time. It seemed so strange. How could me wiping a booger in the family car mean that I don't care about my wife? From my prospective, and I would have to assume that many men see it this way, I was uncomfortable. I had an irritation on my nose, so I reached in and handled it. It wasn't until I had the thing on my finger, and then realized that I was next to my wife, who might be grossed out by what I'd done. Did Mel even cross my mind? Nearly 90% of what I'd done was on impulse. I was irritated, so I picked. Never once did I see what I was doing as a personal attack. I never thought that she might assume that picking my nose translated to me not caring for her.

"What are you talking about?" I asked. "What do you mean I don't care for you? Obviously, I care for you? You are my wife."

Mel turned to look at me. "If you cared for me, you'd care about how gross I think boogers are and you wouldn't wipe them on the seat of my car."

Her glasses started to fall forward. She pushed them back up.

"I am so confused right now," I said. "I had a booger. I picked it because it was uncomfortable. That's it."

"So you admit it," she said.

"Holy crap," I said. "Yes, I admit it. Now please explain to me how picking my nose translates to me not caring for you?"

Mel went on, telling me that picking my nose and wiping it on her car showed her that I didn't care about her car. I didn't care that my booger might end up on her leg or something. She made it sound like what I'd done was as bad as me picking my nose and wiping it directly on her, then laughing. And although I didn't really get the comparison, I knew her well enough to know that she didn't get worked up about nothing. Most of the time she is level headed. It wasn't always this way. During our first few years of marriage, we really had to learn how to choose our battles. But by this stage, I knew that when she was mad, it was because she really needed things to change.

"I still don't understand why you are taking this so personal. But what I will say is that I'm sorry. I didn't realize that it meant this much to you."

Mel thought for a moment. Salem was only a few miles away by now. Both kids slept. Then Mel said, "The problem is that we have been married for a long time, and every time you do something like that, I find you less attractive."

That comment hit hard. And when I think back on it, I can't help but think about how much I've changed since getting married. Mel really has helped me grow into a good husband and father. And I like to think that I have done the same for her. And I must assume that me holding onto the childish habit of picking my nose makes her feel like she is still married to the foul-mouthed 20-something she started out with.

"Do you want me to vacuum the car? Would that help?" I said.

"Yes," she said. "It would."

We drove the rest of the way to Salem without speaking. Once I got home, I vacuumed out the car and thought about my habits and how to break them.

I THOUGHT I WAS A GOOD HUSBAND UNTIL I WENT GROCERY SHOPPING

I hadn't gone to the grocery store alone for five years. This is not to say that I hadn't stepped foot in a grocery store. I'd gone to pick up this or that, some milk and bananas, that sort of thing, and I'd accompanied Mel to the grocery store. But I hadn't been to the store by myself to get groceries, real groceries to last a week or more, in five years.

Mel always did that. I assumed that this had nothing to do with gender roles and everything to do with trust. Mel is a vegetarian. She's the kind of person who cares about where a chicken was raised and how it was fed and whether its feelings were considered when it was turned into dinner. She gets worked up about GMOs and high fructose corn syrup. She cares a great deal about what the family eats.

I don't.

If grocery shopping were my responsibility, I'd come home with some cases of diet soda, a few bags of Tyson's frozen chicken, cereal (bags, not boxes—I like to save money), and some tubes of various bread dough. Because really, that's all I'm interested

211

in eating. I'm a picky eater. Not picky in the way of having high standards, but picky in the way that I only like what most people see as crappy, bland food. I don't really like things with flavor. I'm that guy with the plain cheeseburger—only meat, cheese, and bun. Sometimes bacon. I'm that guy who doesn't put ketchup on his fries. I'm that guy who gags when eating onions. I'm that guy with a pile of peas and carrots picked from the main dish and piled up on the side of his plate like a six-year-old. I'm that guy you assume is strange or an asshole because he clearly doesn't enjoy your cooking.

This drives Mel crazy because she really cares about food. She follows cooking blogs, subscribes to cooking magazines, and has several shelves of cookbooks. It's not unusual for her to show me a glossy magazine photo of a casserole and ask, "Would you eat that, or turn your nose up at it?"

"I'm not eating that."

"Well...I'm going to make it anyways and you are going to love it!"

"No. I won't. What I will do is make a bowl of cereal that night."

But Mel was in a tight spot. She was eight months pregnant, and she liked to do shopping for our family of four only once a month. She was too far along to spend several hours wandering around the store, and she refused to use the Mart-Cart, like I suggested. "I'm not going to be one of those people," she said.

"Can I be one of those people for you?" I asked. "Because I think the Mart-Cart looks like fun."

"No," she said.

This meant that she had to send me, her "I don't give a damn about food" husband, to get groceries. She'd seen this coming, but I think she dreaded it. And, in true Mel fashion, she had prepared for this inevitability by taking me to the store with her the past few months to *train me*. During our training sessions, I followed

Mel around the store, helped keep the kids in line, and kind of zoned out. I just didn't see the point in being trained. Mostly because I was offended by the whole notion. It made me feel that Mel thought I was a moron who couldn't get food from a shelf and place it in a cart.

Before I left for my solo voyage to the store, Mel gave me an organized shopping list with three columns, headers that grouped items based on the aisles in the store, and 71 items.

"Just walk in and go right. Then go through each aisle," she said.

She went through each item on the list explaining what she wanted and where I could find it. I could see concern in her eyes. She believed I was a moron who couldn't do something as simple as go grocery shopping, and I wondered where she came up with this notion. What had I done to lose her trust? I'm sure wiping boogers under the seat of her car didn't help.

"You can trust me," I said.

She let out a long breath. "I hope so."

"I'm not an idiot," I said. "I can go shopping. I mean honestly. What's at stake here if I don't do this right? Are we not going to eat? Are the kids going to die? Are you going to leave me?"

Mel didn't say anything. She just nodded. Slowly. Suspiciously.

Mel insists on driving to Corvallis, a slightly larger town 30 minutes away, because they have a WinCo. She says they have good prices and a bulk section. She also likes the way they pay their employees a living wage.

I made the drive, got my cart, put on my headphones, and brought out my list. I walked into the store with a swagger, feeling confident that I had this.

I'll show her who's an idiot, I thought.

First up: the bulk foods. I found the unbleached flour just fine and the quinoa no problem. Spaghetti, that was easy. But the wild rice, I shit you not, there were four kinds of wild rice in the bulk section.

What the hell? I thought. How could there be four kinds of wild rice? There is wild rice, and there is tame rice…right? Who made all this wild rice? Prisoners?

"Damn it!"

I was forced to call Mel and ask her what rice she preferred. I did the same thing in the Popcorn/Cookies/Candy/Cracker section, and again in the Baking/Spices section.

And in the canned products, my mind was blown when I saw that Mel had four different types of canned tomatoes listed. Somehow I didn't notice this when we went over the list. It was then I started to realize that I was in over my head. I looked around for twenty minutes to find tomatoes diced with green chilies, something that I didn't think really existed, and assumed that Mel put on the list just to screw with me. I almost called Mel again for the tenth time. I should say that Mel was never judgmental or rude about all my many calls. She never said, "See! It's harder than you thought!" or "I told you so" or any of that crap. She always just answered my questions sweetly. But even with her non-judgmental tone, I still felt ashamed by how much I'd had to call her.

Luckily, I happened to run into Dave, a friend who worked with me at the university. He was a slender man in his late 40s with a Ph.D. in education. His office sat two down from mine.

I explained my dilemma, and he helped me to realize that tomatoes diced with green chilies are a real thing. He even told me where to find them.

"You don't shop much, do you?" asked Dave.

"No," I said.

Dave laughed, softly and awkwardly. Then he looked me up and down with suspicion, like I was some kind of chauvinist. Like I was the kind of guy that went to work and did nothing else for his wife. I wanted to explain myself. I wanted to tell him that it wasn't about gender, but about me not caring about what I ate. But I didn't. My argument seemed confused and weightless as I formed it in my mind, and by the time I thought I could actually form a sentence, he'd made his judgment, and we'd said our goodbyes.

As Dave walked away, I started to realize that maybe all this shopping I'd thrown my hands up to over the past five years was about more than just me not caring about what I ate. Maybe it was about me not caring enough about my wife.

I know this sounds dramatic, but Mel really cares about cooking. She gets excited about it, and I have never cared about that. In fact, I don't appreciate it. They say the way to a man's heart is through his stomach, but that isn't the case with me. I just don't get excited about a good meal. But Mel does, and I think she wishes that I did, too. I think she wishes that I cared about what she cooked, that I valued how much time she spent at the store and how much thought she put into her meals, but I didn't.

And I have told her as much.

It's always friendly and with the explanation that it had nothing to do with her and everything to do with the fact that I just don't care about food. Nevertheless, telling her that I don't care about food when she has put so much work into it seems to say that I don't care about her and her passions.

I stood in the aisle and thought about the suspicious look she gave while reviewing the list, and I wondered if perhaps she wasn't assuming that I was an idiot, but rather hoping that I'd appreciate how much time and effort she put into giving our family good food. But instead of complimenting her, I made it about me.

I am an asshole.

I hated these kinds of revelations, and sadly, I seemed to have a lot of them lately.

More than an hour into shopping, I'd called Mel over a dozen times. I started to realize that I looked a lot like all the single men walking the aisles wearing headphones. Most of them had lists, only they weren't nicely organized and on full sheets of paper like mine, but rather messy scrawls on coasters or torn corner sheets of newspaper, that sort of thing. Ready-made dinners from the frozen section filled their carts. This was a college town, so a lot of the men were in their late teens and early 20s. They had a spring in their step and a confident smirk that reminded me of when I was in my early 20s shopping after graduating from high school. I recall feeling like I'd really figured things out. I was an independent adult shopping and living on my own. I had my shit together.

I didn't pay much attention to them.

Who I did pay attention to were the single men in their 30s— the obviously single ones, probably divorced, who held a look of contempt or fear. They were the men who looked at ladies in the store with longing and hope that they might find something of value in their sad carts filled with cases of diet soda, a few bags of Tyson's frozen chicken, bags of cereal, and tubes of various bread dough. They looked so sad and lonely, and I had complete empathy for them.

One guy had a serious neck beard and greasy bleached hair with dark roots. He wore a wrinkled Call of Duty T-shirt and an old pair of wide-legged Jinco Jeans from the late 90s.

He looked a lot like I did before meeting my wife.

He was in his mid-30s, wasn't wearing a ring, and was pushing a cart full of TV dinners. Perhaps this guy was single because he wanted to be. Perhaps he was just like me and had an 8-month pregnant wife at home and was grocery shopping for the first time in five years. Perhaps my assumption that he was a single straight man, wandering the grocery store, lonely and sad, was incorrect. I don't know anything about him except for what I observed. But what I do know is that as I looked at his sad eyes and sad diet and sad list written on a torn piece of cardboard that appeared to come off a box of cereal, I wanted to give him hug.

I looked at him and saw myself as a single man in my 30s, and I got really scared and felt ever so grateful for my wife, her grocery list, the ways she doesn't let me wipe boogers under the seat and doesn't let me leave the toilet clogged up. Even though these things are annoying sometimes, I'd rather have them with her in my life than not have them and not have her. And here is the really scary part. The middle-aged women shopping in the store seemed to assume that I was one of these lonely single men. This meant that they wouldn't make eye contact with me. If I glanced in their direction, they looked right at the ground or to the side or their lists. I felt like this thing that was not good enough to look at.

There might be good explanations for this. Perhaps these women were happily married or in a happy relationship with someone, and they didn't want to put across the wrong idea. Maybe they just weren't looking for a relationship. Perhaps they simply weren't into short, stocky white guys with a shaved head and a trimmed beard. But as they looked away, it made me think about the way Mel looks right at me and smiles. The way her eyes light up when she sees me.

I stopped, right there, in the frozen aisle, and gave Mel another call. She picked up and I said, "Stop calling me."

"You called me, ya jerk."

"Yeah. You're right. I am a jerk."

I told her about the tomatoes with green chilies, about how I was over my head, and how the store was filled with lonely, single men.. I told her about how the women were looking away from me like I was bad fruit.

"I just want you to know that I love you, and that I appreciate all the work you put into planning our meals. I love the way you look at me, and I am grateful that you have put up with my shit for this long. You are amazing. I'm sorry for not appreciating this earlier."

Maybe it didn't come out quite that smoothly, and maybe I stumbled a little bit in what I had to say, and perhaps Mel had to ask me to repeat certain parts because I was taking softly so the people around me wouldn't hear. But that is the gist of what I said, and it came from the heart, and Mel replied by saying, "I love you, too. Thank you."

I can only assume that the people listening to this conversation in the store thought I was a crazy ranting man, and perhaps I was, but this experience reminded me of how much I value Mel and what she does for me, and sometimes, when things like this happen, I find it best to just pick up the phone and let Mel know how much I appreciate her. I suppose that's what I've learned to do after ten years of kids and messy houses and viruses and sleepless nights and all the other maddens that can happen with marriage and family. It can all be crazy sometimes, but there is so much love there, too. I wouldn't give it up for anything, and making sure that my wife knows I appreciate her is the real key to making a family work.

I grabbed the last dozen or so items. Altogether I'd been shopping for three hours. My legs hurt, but I felt enlightened. I came home and hauled all the bags in, which took much longer than I expected and made my arms tired.

Mel was in the kitchen putting things away. I gave her a kiss. Told her again that I loved her and all that she did. She smiled and asked, "Where are the lemons? I need them for dinner."

I thought about it for a moment. I didn't recall picking up any lemons. I looked at the list, and sure enough, I saw them on the list. But I hadn't put a line through them.

"Looks like I missed them."

Mel exhaled and rolled her eyes.

I put my jacket on again and headed back to the store.

ACKNOWLEDGMENTS

First and foremost, Melodie Edwards. Thank you for reading my work and for letting me write so openly about our lives.

Thank you to the very talented writing instructors at Utah Valley University for giving me my creative beginnings: Karin Anderson, Stephen Fullmer, Lee Mortensen, Scott Hatch, and Kathryn McPherson.

Thank you to the MFA faculty at Minnesota State University, Mankato for your influence and support: Geoff Herbach, Candace Black, Diana Joseph, Richard Robbins, Roger Sheffer, and Richard Terrill.

I am much obliged to Kara Balcerzak, Caitlin O'Sullivan, Sarah Johnson, Amber Watson, Jimmy Neel, Heather Hadley, Elizabeth Christianson, Melody Heide, Loz Cook, Brandon Henderson, and The Greens, for reading draft after draft of my shitty writing.

I'm lucky to have such amazing followers of *No Idea What I'm Doing: A Daddy Blog.* You keep me going.

Mom, Melissa, Ryan, and Kip (my fam): I know you don't really understand why I write, but thank you for trying to understand.

Tristan, Norah, and Aspen. You give me all my material. Please continue to keep it real. I love you.

Made in the USA
Lexington, KY
08 January 2016